Y0-BDJ-170

DISCARDED BY

MT LEBANON PUBLIC LIBRARY

FORENSICS

UNCOVER THE SCIENCE AND TECHNOLOGY OF CRIME SCENE INVESTIGATION

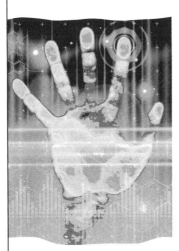

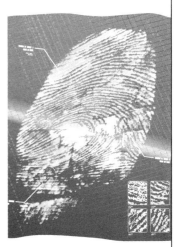

Mt. Lebanon Public Library
16 Castle Shannon Boulevard
Pittsburgh, PA 15228-2252
412-531-1912
www.mtlebanonlibrary.org

Carla Mooney

Illustrated by
Samuel Carbaugh

~ Titles in the *Inquire and Investigate* Series ~

MT. LEBANON PUBLIC LIBRARY

NOV 1 7 2014

 **green press INITIATIVE**

Nomad Press is committed to preserving ancient forests and natural resources. We elected to print *Forensics: Uncover the Science and Technology of Crime Scene Investigation* on Thor PCW containing 30% post consumer waste.

Nomad Press made this paper choice because our printer, Sheridan Books, is a member of Green Press Initiative, a nonprofit program dedicated to supporting authors, publishers, and suppliers in their efforts to reduce their use of fiber obtained from endangered forests.

For more information, visit www.greenpressinitiative.org.

Nomad Press
A division of Nomad Communications
10 9 8 7 6 5 4 3 2 1

Copyright © 2013 by Nomad Press. All rights reserved.
No part of this book may be reproduced in any form without permission in writing from
the publisher, except by a reviewer who may quote brief passages in a review or **for limited educational use**.
The trademark "Nomad Press" and the Nomad Press logo are trademarks of Nomad Communications, Inc.

This book was manufactured by Sheridan Books, Ann Arbor, MI USA.
July 2013, Job #**348215**
ISBN: 978-1-61930-184-9

Illustrations by Samuel
Educational Consultant, Marla Conn

Questions regarding the ordering of this book should be addressed to
Independent Publishers Group
814 N. Franklin St.
Chicago, IL 60610
www.ipgbook.com

Nomad Press
2456 Christian St.
White River Junction, VT 05001
www.nomadpress.net

Contents ▶

▾ TIMELINE

44 BCE .... Antistius, a Roman physician, performs the first recorded autopsy on Julius Caesar.

700 CE .... The Chinese use fingerprints to establish the identity of documents and clay sculptures.

1149 .... King Richard of England introduces the idea of a coroner to investigate questionable deaths.

1248 .... The first written account of forensic science being used to solve crimes is recorded in the book *Xi Juan Ji Lu* (*Collected Cases of Injustice Rectified*) by Song Ci, a judge in the Chinese criminal court.

1540s .... Dr. Ambroise Paré, a French army surgeon, systematically studies the effect of violent death on internal organs. His work is the beginning of modern forensic pathology.

1784 .... The first case of physical matching occurs in England when John Toms is tried and convicted of murdering Edward Culshaw with a pistol. A pistol wad—crushed paper used to secure gunpowder and balls in a pistol's muzzle—that is found in Culshaw's head wound matches perfectly with a torn newspaper in Toms's possession.

1820s .... French detective Eugène François Vidocq studies bullets to identify murder weapons and makes plaster casts of shoe impressions to solve crimes.

1835 .... Sir Henry Goddard of London's Scotland Yard police uses physical analysis to match a bullet to a gun.

1836 .... Scottish chemist James Marsh develops a chemical test to detect the presence of arsenic, which is used in a murder trial.

1864 .... Odelbrecht advocates the use of photography to identify criminals and document evidence at crime scenes.

1891 .... Dr. Juan Vucetich of Argentina creates the first fingerprint classification system, which is still used in Spanish-speaking countries.

1892 .... Sir Francis Galton publishes *Finger Prints*, the first book on the subject. He develops pattern types and demonstrates that no two prints are identical.

▾ THE HISTORY OF FORENSICS

1896............ Sir Edward Richard Henry from England develops a fingerprint classification system that becomes standard in English-speaking countries.

1910............ Dr. Edmond Locard founds the first laboratory in France dedicated to criminal investigation. He later becomes famous for his principle, "Every contact leaves a trace."

1920s........... Dr. Calvin Goddard, a physician and expert in firearms identification, uses the comparison microscope to identify which bullets came from which shell casings.

1924............ August Vollmer, chief of the Los Angeles Police Department, establishes the first American police crime laboratory.

1930............ Karl Landsteiner wins the Nobel Prize for classifying human blood into groups A, B, AB, and O.

1933............ The Federal Bureau of Investigation's crime lab is created.

1937............ Luminol is found to react with the hemoglobin in blood and produce a bluish glow.

1953............ James Watson and Francis Crick discover the DNA double helix, which will become the basis for DNA fingerprinting in forensic science.

1970............ The FBI introduces the beginnings of the Automated Fingerprint Identification System.

1984............ Sir Alec Jeffreys of England develops the first DNA fingerprinting tests for use in a criminal case.

1990s........... The FBI starts to build its Combined DNA Index System (CODIS), the first computerized nationwide system for matching DNA samples from suspects with those collected from crime scenes. It will become the largest DNA data bank in the world.

2012............ Digital image enhancements allow investigators to better match details such as fingerprints, shoe prints, and bite marks.

2012............ New DNA technology allows for forensic testing of older and smaller samples.

Introduction▶
Crack the Case

How do police
and investigators
solve crimes?

>> Investigators use science to solve crimes and bring criminals to justice.

FORENSIC FACT

Sir Arthur Conan Doyle's Sherlock Holmes is one of the earliest and most famous fictional forensic scientists.

Have you ever wondered how the police and investigators solve crimes?

For most of history, police relied on eyewitnesses to help them figure out who committed a crime. If an eyewitness saw a thief breaking into a store, he or she identified the criminal to police. If no one caught the criminal in the act, the crime often remained unsolved. But even when there were witnesses to a crime, their testimony was not always reliable. Sometimes witnesses contradicted each other. Sometimes they changed their stories. Sometimes they were simply wrong.

As technology has improved in the last century, investigators have relied less on eyewitnesses and more on science to tell the story of a crime. Better cameras snap more detailed crime scene pictures. Microscopes allow scientists to examine and identify the tiniest pieces of evidence. Understanding DNA and blood typing has created ways to tie a suspect to a crime scene without an eyewitness.

Today, no one needs to catch a criminal in the act in order to solve a crime. The tools and techniques of science allow investigators to track down a criminal long after he or she has left the crime scene.

WHAT IS FORENSICS?

Every time a crime is committed, a criminal leaves evidence at the scene. Forensics is the science of finding that evidence and analyzing it for clues. Evidence may be a large bloody footprint or a microscopic carpet fiber. A criminal might leave a fingerprint, a strand of hair, or a broken window.

Each piece of evidence reveals a clue about what happened at the scene. Using scientific tools and principles, forensic scientists make careful observations and analyze evidence found at the crime scene. Then they present evidence in court to prove a defendant's guilt or innocence.

CRACK THE CASE

The activities in *Forensics: Uncover the Science and Technology of Crime Scene Investigation* will introduce you to the skills and techniques used by forensic scientists to uncover evidence, recreate a crime, and follow the trail to a criminal. Like forensic scientists, you will apply concepts of biology, anatomy, chemistry, and physics to analyze crime scene evidence. You will discover how forensic scientists use evidence to develop and support hypotheses about a crime.

During your investigations, you will learn how to use science to crack the case.

>> There is a lot of new vocabulary in this book! Turn to the glossary in the back when you come to a word you don't understand.

FROM THE LATIN WORD

Forensics is the science of finding and analyzing crime scene evidence. The word *forensic* comes from the Latin word *forum*, which means "public" or "to share with the public." In ancient Rome, a person accused of a crime and the accuser would each tell their side of the story to a group of people in a public forum. The person who made the best argument won the case.

Chapter 1 ▶
The World of Forensics

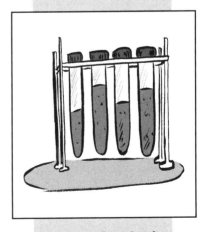

What is the role of forensic science?

A dead body lies on the ground. A priceless necklace has disappeared from a jewelry store. A house burns down after its owner receives a threatening letter. In each of these scenarios, the police are called to the crime scene. Now it's their job to answer the question—what happened here?

THE SCENE OF THE CRIME

The primary crime scene is the original location of a crime or accident. The crime scene is different for each crime. It can be a room, a house, the surrounding property, or even an entire neighborhood. At a minimum, the crime scene must include the exact spot where a crime took place. It must also include areas where the site can be entered or exited.

Sometimes key pieces of evidence are found outside the primary crime scene. A dropped gun or muddy footprint may be found in another room or down the street. These alternate locations are secondary crime scenes.

FORENSIC FACT

The first crime lab was founded in 1924 by August Vollmer at the Los Angeles Police Department.

Police officers are usually the first to arrive at a crime scene. The police assess the scene and answer questions such as "Did a crime occur here?" Then they determine "What type of crime?" and "Where exactly did the crime occur?" They follow a strict set of procedures to ensure no evidence at the scene is lost, damaged, or contaminated. To prevent damage, police secure the crime scene. They mark the perimeter of the scene and block access with bright yellow police tape that bears a printed warning such as "CRIME SCENE DO NOT CROSS." Police detectives also interview people in the area who may be eyewitnesses or persons of interest in the crime.

THE FORENSIC TEAM

Who looks at the evidence? After the police secure the crime scene, they call in crime scene specialists. In larger cities, the forensic team may include specialists who focus on one specific aspect of the crime scene such as fingerprints or tool marks. In smaller cities, the forensic team may be only a few people who perform multiple roles and functions, or even a single officer. Forensic scientists are usually not police officers.

In larger regions, the forensic team may have a special crime scene investigation (CSI) unit. The members of the CSI unit are trained to recognize, collect, and preserve evidence at a crime scene. When called to the scene, they search for, collect, and document items such as fibers, glass fragments, and blood spatter. CSI photographers take pictures of the entire area and close shots of specific pieces of evidence. If the CSI unit discovers evidence that should be handled by an expert, they may call in specialists such as forensic entomologists, who analyze insects, or forensic anthropologists, who recover and examine human remains to help identify a person.

❯❯ Members of the forensic team do not carry guns, question witnesses, or make arrests. Instead, they specialize in collecting and analyzing evidence.

Evidence can be direct or circumstantial. Direct evidence establishes a fact. It can be an eyewitness statement or a confession from a suspect. Circumstantial evidence requires a person to make an inference about what happened. For example, if a fingerprint found at the crime scene matches the suspect, the investigator may infer that it links the suspect to the crime. While a great deal of evidence obtained by forensic scientists is circumstantial, it can be used in courts to determine guilt or innocence.

>> Evidence at a crime scene is like a piece of a larger puzzle. Investigators fit the pieces together to create a picture of the crime.

Sometimes, a district attorney and medical examiner may be called to a crime scene. The district attorney can issue a search warrant if police detectives need to follow up on a lead discovered at the crime scene. When a body is found, the medical examiner can examine it and determine a preliminary cause of death.

PUZZLE PIECES OF THE CRIME

Forensic scientists search crime scenes to find evidence, and then they analyze it to determine how it fits into the overall picture. Evidence can help the investigative team recreate what happened at a crime scene. It can also lead them to a suspect and link him or her to the crime scene. For example, if investigators find a suspect's fingerprints at the scene, they can reasonably infer that the suspect was present at the scene. In court, the prosecutor presents the forensic evidence to the jury to support a case against a defendant.

Evidence can prove that a crime has been committed or help investigators understand a crime's key elements. Using blood spatter patterns, investigators may be able to recreate the movements of people at the crime scene. Evidence such as DNA or fingerprints may also help investigators discover the identity of a victim or suspect. It may also link a suspect to a crime scene or a victim.

In some cases, evidence supports a suspect who claims to be innocent. For example, if DNA evidence found at the crime scene does not match the suspect's DNA, investigators may need to search for another person. Evidence may also provide clues for detectives to follow as they investigate the crime.

TYPES OF EVIDENCE

Evidence at a crime scene can take many forms.

- **Testimonial evidence** includes oral or written statements from eyewitnesses.

- **Physical evidence** includes what is found at the crime scene, on a victim, or in a suspect's possession. Physical evidence can include fingerprints, documents, glass fragments, bullets, and shell casings. It also includes biological and trace evidence.

- **Biological evidence** includes organic items such as blood, saliva, hair, plants, and insects.

- **Trace evidence** includes very small but measurable objects such as hair strands, fibers, or skin cells. Some trace evidence is also biological evidence.

Some types of evidence are more reliable than others. Physical evidence such as fingerprints and biological evidence such as DNA strongly link a suspect to a crime scene. On the other hand, eyewitness testimony can frequently be wrong, making it a weaker link.

Evidence can also be reconstructive or associative. Reconstructive evidence answers the questions of who, what, where, how, and when and helps investigators piece together the event. Broken glass or door locks may show where a criminal entered and exited the scene of the crime. Footprints and bullet trajectories may determine where everyone was located and how the sequence of events unfolded. Blood spatter may reveal clues about how the victim was attacked or how quickly he or she died.

Associative evidence links a suspect to the crime scene. Fingerprints, footprints, hair, fibers, blood, and other objects and substances prove that a suspect was at the scene. Associative evidence can prove that someone other than the suspect was present at the crime scene.

CLASS VS. INDIVIDUAL EVIDENCE

Evidence can have class or individual characteristics. Identifying the size and manufacturer of a tire that made a tire track is an example of class evidence. If a suspect's car has different tires, this piece of class evidence may exclude their car. Identifying a particular tire with certain wear patterns is the kind of individual evidence that can ID a suspect and place them at the crime scene.

>> **Evidence collected at a crime scene can answer many questions. Reconstructive evidence helps investigators piece together the event. Associative evidence links people to the crime scene.**

FORENSIC FACT

An investigator may scratch his or her initials into bullet shell casings found at the crime scene so that he or she can identify the casing in court.

Processing a crime scene is a long, tedious process. The CSI team documents the conditions at the scene and collects any evidence that might be a clue to what happened and who was involved. A CSI might collect dried blood drops, cast tool-mark impressions, pick fibers from a victim's shirt, or scrape cells from underneath a victim's fingernails. At the same time, the CSI ensures that all the evidence is safely collected and preserved. If evidence is contaminated or damaged before the crime lab analyzes it, the lab may never be able to identify it or link it to a suspect.

When the CSI team arrives at a crime scene, they first interview the police officer at the scene to determine what is already known about the crime, who did it, and how it happened. The CSI team also checks to make sure the police have secured the crime scene.

Protecting the crime scene is based on Locard's Exchange Principle. Every person who enters the scene may take away key trace evidence, while at the same time leaving behind traces of their presence that interfere with the CSI's investigation. The CSI interviews police to determine who has entered or exited the crime scene and if any objects were moved.

Then the CSI carefully examines and walks through the crime scene to get a general idea of the area and its layout. The walk-through helps the CSI identify possible points of entry and exit from the crime scene. Throughout the walk-through, the CSI is extremely careful not to disturb or touch anything.

Next, the CSI documents everything at the crime scene, using detailed notes, sketches, photographs, and video. The CSI's documentation includes an overall description of the crime scene and a list of possible evidence. He or she photographs and sketches the overall scene, showing each piece of evidence in relation to the others. Investigators will also measure and record the distance of each piece of evidence from two fixed points such as a wall, tree, or sidewalk.

The investigator systematically searches the area, usually moving in a geometric pattern to make sure no inch of the scene is missed. In an evidence log, the CSI describes each piece, and records when, where, and by whom it was found as well as who transported it to the crime lab. Each potential piece of evidence is tagged, photographed, and packaged so it can be sent back to the lab.

The CSI will photograph objects, lift fingerprints, and cast or photograph impressions of tool marks. To find trace fibers and stains, the CSI may use an alternate light source and tweezers. The investigator may also vacuum carpet and furniture in the crime scene for trace evidence that escapes the investigator's eye. As the scene is processed, the CSI packages each piece of evidence separately to preserve it and prevent damage. CSIs use envelopes, canisters, bottles, and paper and plastic bags to package evidence. For liquid evidence, the CSI may choose an unbreakable airtight container. For moist or wet evidence, the CSI may use a container with airflow that allows the evidence to dry out.

LOCARD'S EXCHANGE PRINCIPLE

Forensic science is based upon Locard's Exchange Principle. Dr. Edmond Locard (1877–1966) was a French police officer who worked as a medical examiner during World War I. In 1910, he opened the world's first crime investigation lab in Lyons, France. Locard believed that when two items make contact, they exchange a piece of their materials. In other words, when you travel somewhere, you leave a little piece of yourself behind. At the same time, you pick up a little piece of wherever you have been.

>> **After documenting the overall crime scene, the investigator is ready to find, document, and preserve specific pieces of evidence.**

A criminal will leave some trace of himself or herself at a crime scene. These traces may be fingerprints, footprints, hair, skin, blood, fluids, soil, and more. At the same time, a criminal coming into contact with objects at the crime scene will take away part of the scene, such as dirt, fibers, or other trace evidence. This exchange of materials is the basis of modern forensic science. Forensic scientists scour and analyze a crime scene looking for traces left by a suspect or traces picked up by a suspect that could link him or her to the crime scene.

>> If there is an error in the chain of custody documentation, a court may rule that the evidence could have been damaged or contaminated and therefore cannot be used at trial.

In addition to collecting evidence, the CSI also gathers control samples from the crime scene. A control sample is something like a hair, fiber, or fingerprint from a known source. The crime lab will compare the control sample against evidence found at the crime scene. For example, hairs found on a victim's jacket may be compared to hairs from the victim's own head, and the hairs of other people who live in the victim's house. If the hair does not match any of the control samples, the investigators know they have discovered a potential clue that may help identify the criminal.

While collecting crime scene evidence, investigators are careful to follow and document a chain of custody for each piece of evidence. The chain of custody is a continuous record that shows every person who has touched evidence from the time it is discovered at the crime scene, while it is collected and transported to the crime lab, and until it is processed at the lab. Every person who handles a piece of evidence must be documented in the chain of custody record.

DEVELOP A HYPOTHESIS

While the forensic team searches the crime scene and processes the evidence, they develop an initial working hypothesis of the crime. What happened here? In what order did the events happen?

Based on the position of evidence, the team develops an idea of who was at the scene and where they were. They build a theory about the sequence of events. The team considers each new piece of evidence. Does it support their hypothesis of the crime? If yes, the initial hypothesis becomes stronger. However, if investigators find evidence that does not fit the hypothesis, the team must rethink their theory and adjust it to fit the new evidence.

AT THE CRIME LAB

The crime lab processes evidence collected by investigators at the crime scene. Small local labs are usually equipped for basic testing and analysis. Larger regional and state crime labs often offer more services and testing, while the FBI Laboratory performs almost every forensic test available. The FBI Laboratory also maintains databases of items such as fingerprints and DNA that investigators around the country may use.

At a lab, forensic scientists perform a variety of tests.

- **Drug chemistry** tests identify the presence of legal and illegal drugs.

- **Trace chemistry** tests compare and identify materials left from fires, explosions, and paints.

- **Latent prints** are processed to compare fingerprints recovered at the crime scene to individuals.

- **Microscopic examination** compares and analyzes hairs, fibers, soils, and other materials.

- **Firearms tests** compare guns, fired bullets, and gunpowder patterns.

- **Documents** found at the scene are examined to identify handwriting, ink, paper, printers, and other characteristics that would help locate its source.

Each test helps investigators build a clearer picture of what happened at the crime scene.

FORENSIC FACT

Calvin Goddard, founder of the first private forensic lab in Chicago in 1929, helped the Federal Bureau of Investigation establish a national forensic lab in 1932. Today, the FBI Laboratory offers a wide range of forensic and analysis services to law enforcement departments across the United States and has become a model for state and local crime labs.

DOCUMENT A CRIME SCENE

When a crime occurs, a detailed and accurate documentation of the crime scene allows forensic scientists to recreate the scene, test theories, and reconstruct the events that occurred.

Crime scene investigators photograph, videotape, and make sketches of the scene. They measure the location of key pieces of evidence in relation to fixed objects such as walls, trees, or lampposts. As CSIs process the crime scene, they also formulate a working hypothesis as to the events that occurred at the scene. Working with your teacher, classmates, parent, or on your own, you can create your own crime scene. Then you will become a CSI and examine and document the evidence at your scene.

- **Have a teacher, parent, or member of your group gather pieces of evidence and place them in various locations in the area you have chosen to be your crime scene (a classroom, family room, outdoor location).** Upon arriving at the crime scene, what do you notice? How can you record the overall crime scene?

- **Carefully walk through your crime scene and identify possible pieces of evidence.** Place numbered, folded index cards next to each piece of evidence to identify it. Is there any evidence you want to photograph or sketch separately? Since size is important, you should place a ruler next to the evidence in your photograph or sketch. Make sure each piece of marked evidence is included in your overall sketch of the crime scene.

- **Create an evidence and photo log.** The log should list each piece of evidence, its assigned number, its description, and its location from two fixed points. The photo log should describe each photo in sequence.

- simulated pieces of evidence such as a glove, shoe print, note, fingerprints, discarded glasses, dirt
- paper and pencil
- 3-by-5 index cards
- camera
- ruler
- tape measure

Object	Description	Fixed Point 1	Fixed Point 2
1	Glove on left arm of couch	Window frame left side: 36 inches	Fireplace right side: 49 inches

- **Measure the location of each piece of evidence from two fixed points in the room.** Note that most furniture can be moved and would not be considered a fixed point in a room. Add these measurements to your evidence log.

After you have completed documenting the crime scene, think about what might have happened to explain the scene. What was the crime? How do you account for the position of the various pieces of evidence? What is your initial working hypothesis of the crime? How does each piece of evidence support or contradict your hypothesis? Now go back and look again. Do you notice anything you missed before? Does this change your hypothesis?

HOW ACCURATE IS YOUR EYEWITNESS?

At a crime scene, investigators try to interview eyewitnesses who may have seen the crime taking place. Eyewitness accounts can be helpful to investigators when analyzing a crime scene, even though investigators know that eyewitness accounts can often be inaccurate. Two people who view the same event may have different accounts depending on their position, line of sight, and other conditions that may affect their perception and memory.

You can test how well people remember the details from a crime scene by creating your own scene and then comparing the eyewitness testimony from several viewers.

- **Using a video camera and several friends, film a short video of a simple crime.** For example, your friends could pretend to be walking down the street and a "thief" could come by and snatch a purse or other object from one of them.

- **Create a written list of questions that a police investigator would ask an eyewitness to the crime.** Ideas include:

    a. Describe what you saw.

    b. Was the criminal male or female?

    c. What was the criminal wearing?

    d. Approximately how tall was the criminal?

    e. Give a general description of the criminal.

- **Assemble a group of volunteers to watch your video without knowing what they will see.** After the volunteers watch the video, question each volunteer individually. Half of them should answer the questions immediately. Have the second group answer the questions several hours later.

- **Compare the answers from each eyewitness. How many answered the questions correctly?** Which questions were most likely to be answered correctly or incorrectly? How did the responses from each group differ?

To investigate more, create different versions of your video—use different lighting, have the criminal wear different clothing or appear on screen for shorter or longer periods, or film from a different distance or angle. How do these changes affect your eyewitness testimony? You may also change the amount of time between watching the video and answering the questions. How does this affect eyewitness testimony?

Ideas for Supplies ▼

- video camera
- several friends or classmates
- television or computer for video playback
- several eyewitness volunteers
- paper and pencils

Chapter 2▶
Fingerprints

How are fingerprints
found and used to
solve a crime?

>> A fingerprint can provide a key piece of evidence prosecutors need to tie the thief to the crime.

FORENSIC FACT

Ancient Chinese and Babylonian civilizations used fingerprints to sign legal documents.

What if a thief stole a valuable necklace and is nowhere to be found? What if there were no witnesses and no video surveillance cameras captured the thief's identity?

It's up to investigators to figure out what happened. At the crime scene, they examine every door handle, windowsill, piece of furniture, and object in the room. Somewhere, the thief may have left a fingerprint or other clues to his or her identity.

WHAT ARE FINGERPRINTS?

Look at your fingers. Everyone's fingertips are covered in very fine lines that curve, circle, and arch. The raised lines are called friction ridges and the narrow valleys between the ridges are called grooves. Ridges and grooves create a pattern that makes a fingerprint. When you touch a surface or an object, oils, perspiration, and amino acids in the ridges transfer your fingerprint to the surface.

Fingerprints are unique. You'll never find another person with the same fingerprints as yours. Even identical twins with the same DNA have different fingerprints. And fingerprints never change. The prints you have at birth are the same ones you will have when you die. Only a scar can change your fingerprint pattern, but even that will be your own.

Because fingerprints are unique throughout a person's lifetime, they are a powerful tool to identify a victim or suspect. Fingerprint collection, filing, and retrieval are an important part of crime scene processing. Fingerprints found by investigators are often a major part of evidence at a criminal trial. If a fingerprint found at a crime scene matches a suspect's fingerprints, it is a strong piece of evidence linking the suspect to the crime. If fingerprints at the scene do not match a suspect's prints, investigators may decide they're focusing on the wrong person and take a new look at the evidence.

FINDING FINGERPRINTS

Fingerprints can be found on furniture, glass, doorknobs, soap, or even a stick of butter! Patent prints and impressed prints are the easiest fingerprints for investigators to find and document because these are the ones they can see. When someone touches a substance such as blood, ink, paint, dirt, or grease, they often leave behind an obvious patent print. These prints are two-dimensional.

Impressed prints, also called plastic prints, are three-dimensional. When a person touches a soft substance such as wax, putty, soap, butter, or dust, it leaves a 3-D print. Because they are visible, both patent and plastic prints can be photographed easily.

>> Like the treads on a tire, friction ridges give your fingers traction to help you grip objects securely.

Criminals have tried to hide their identity by burning or shaving off their finger pads, but it doesn't work. Their prints disappear for a period of time, but eventually the skin repairs itself and the prints reappear in their original pattern.

FORENSIC FACT

Dactyloscopy is the study of fingerprint identification. A dactylogram is another word for fingerprint.

>> When you ink your fingers and press on a piece of paper, you are creating a patent print.

Ridgeology is the collection and analysis of prints from any section of volar skin, which includes skin on the palms, fingers, toes, and the soles of the feet.

AUTOMATED FINGERPRINT IDENTIFICATION SYSTEM

The Automated Fingerprint Identification System (AFIS) is a computerized system that assists investigators with unknown recovered prints. When investigators recover a print from a crime scene, they can enter it into the AFIS. The database compares the print pattern against others stored in the database, searching for a possible match. When it preliminarily finds one, forensic scientists work to verify the identity of the victim or suspect.

More commonly, fingerprints at a crime scene are latent, or invisible. Latent fingerprints are made from oils, perspiration, and other substances released from pores on the skin. Latent prints cannot be seen with the naked eye. Investigators need to make these prints visible before they can photograph or capture them as evidence. To do this, crime scene investigators use special lighting or processing to find the prints. Hard surfaces are usually the best places to find latent prints, so investigators pay close attention to weapons, tools, furniture, doors, and windows at a crime scene.

One simple trick they use is to angle a flashlight over a surface to see the print. Special laser or ultraviolet lights also cause ridge patterns to pop into view.

Fingerprint technicians may also dust an area for prints. Special powders stick to the oil and residue left behind and highlight a print's ridge pattern. These powders come in many different colors, so investigators choose the color that will contrast the most against the surface they are testing. For example, a white powder may best reveal a print on a black countertop. Fluorescent powders work better to find latent prints on multi-colored surfaces.

When powders won't stick to a surface, such as a plastic bag or plastic container, magnetic powders are used to reveal latent prints. Magnetic powder is also a better choice on textured surfaces that have grooves. Regular powder just falls in the grooves and doesn't show the ridges.

Sometimes investigators need to use chemical techniques to find or enhance latent prints. Ninhydrin is a chemical that bonds with a fingerprint's amino acids, producing a blue or purple color. Investigators use it to find fingerprints on paper or cardboard surfaces. Cyanoacrylate fuming, also known as super glue fuming, is another type of chemical process used to develop latent prints on a variety of objects. The super glue reacts with the amino acids and fatty acids in the latent fingerprint to produce a visible, white material on the print's ridges. Investigators can then photograph and record the print's visible image.

RECOVERING PRINTS

Once they have a visible print, investigators document its location at the crime scene and recover it. One way to recover a print is to photograph it. Fingerprint photographs can be digitally enhanced and scanned into fingerprint databases like the AFIS. Investigators can search the database to find a possible match. The print is also recorded for future searches and matches.

Next, investigators recover a latent print by lifting it. Lifting is done by gently laying the sticky side of a piece of transparent tape over the print and carefully peeling it off. With the print pattern now stuck on the tape, the investigator sticks the tape onto a card so it can be saved and examined later. The lifted print on the card can also be scanned into a digital image. Lifting a print without damaging it is a very delicate process, as the print can easily be smeared.

>> Certain chemicals react with one or more of the substances in latent fingerprints, turning the fingerprint visible.

>> There is no international standard for how many points of similarity are needed to say that one fingerprint matches another. In the United States, prints with as few as eight points of similarity have been called a match.

FORENSIC FACT

Notorious bank robber John Dillinger scarred his fingertips with acid in an attempt to conceal his identity. After FBI agents killed him outside a Chicago theater, they were still able to match his prints with ones on file.

FINGERPRINT PATTERNS

Once a good print has been recovered, a fingerprint examiner examines it. All fingerprints follow one of three basic patterns: arches, loops, and whorls. This is called level 1 detail. A set of fingerprints may include one or more of the three patterns. You might have, for example, one arch, three loops, and one whorl on one hand. Within each category there are subgroups that make up eight main fingerprint patterns:

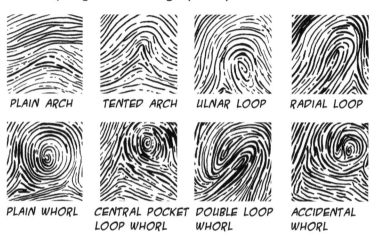

PLAIN ARCH   TENTED ARCH   ULNAR LOOP   RADIAL LOOP

PLAIN WHORL   CENTRAL POCKET LOOP WHORL   DOUBLE LOOP WHORL   ACCIDENTAL WHORL

An arch is the simplest type of fingerprint pattern, but also the most rare. Only about 5 percent of the population has arch prints. Arch patterns have ridges that begin on one side and end on the other side, making a line that looks like a hill. A tented arch has a higher, more prominent spike in the center.

Loop patterns are the most common. They're found in about 70 percent of the population. In a loop pattern, ridges begin and end on the same side. Radial loops start and end on the thumb side of the finger and point toward the radius bone in the forearm. Ulnar loops start and end on the same side as the pinky finger and point toward the forearm's ulna bone. In every loop there is a triangular-shaped pattern like the Greek letter delta (Δ) where fingerprint ridges meet.

In a whorl pattern, the ridges form a spiral that appears to complete a full circle. Approximately 25 percent of the population has whorl prints. There are four major whorl patterns and each one has at least two deltas. Plain whorls have one or more ridges that make a complete circle. You'll see a small circle in the middle with concentric circles spreading out from there. There are two deltas on the print that are on opposite sides of the circles. An imaginary line between the two deltas crosses through some part of the ridge circle.

If the line does not touch the circular ridge pattern at all, the whorl is a central pocket loop. A double loop whorl has two loops combined into one print. It resembles a yin-yang symbol with two teardrop-shaped halves. If a print has two or more patterns or does not fall clearly into any other category, it is considered an accidental whorl.

IDENTIFYING PRINTS

Once a fingerprint has been classified into a pattern group, experts will look at its minutiae points, the level 2 detail. These are the places in the fingerprint pattern where ridges end or two ridges meet. Minutiae points help fingerprint experts identify prints more precisely and compare them against other prints found at the crime scene and against the fingerprint database.

When minutiae points on two different prints match, it is called a point of similarity. If there are many points of similarity between two prints, the examiner may include or exclude individuals. The next phase of the examination of included prints examines the level 3 details—ridge structure, defects such as scars, and sweat pores—to facilitate the identification.

* balloons
* stamp ink pad
* magnifying glass
* fingerprint
  pattern chart
  (available online
  at sciencespot.net/
  Media/FrnsScience/
  fingerprintguide.pdf)

IDENTIFY YOUR OWN
FINGERPRINT PATTERNS

Like a forensic scientist, you can examine your own fingerprints and find the marks and patterns that make you unique. Figure out how many of each pattern type you have among all 10 of your fingers.

* **Start by blowing up a balloon halfway, but don't tie it.** Then ink up your fingers and press each of your finger pads onto the balloon. What happens when you fully inflate the balloon and tie it closed. Can you see the ridge patterns and other characteristics?

* **Study your fingerprints using a magnifying glass if needed to see minutiae points.** Compare them against the fingerprint pattern chart on page 24. What do you see in your fingerprints? Are there any patterns? What do you notice when you look at your fingerprints through a magnifying glass? What different patterns do you have? Are the patterns hard to determine?

To investigate more, compare your fingerprints to those of a friend or another person in your family. What similarities and differences do you find? Do you need to look at minutiae points to tell some of the prints apart?

LIFTING FINGERPRINTS

When forensic scientists find fingerprints at a crime scene, they carefully lift and record the prints to examine and compare them to other prints at the crime lab. With a few tools, you can practice the techniques forensic scientists use to find and lift fingerprints.

- **What happens when you press your fingertip on the clear, hard surface of a CD case or another hard, flat surface?** You might want to try this on both a clear surface and a dark surface to see what happens.

- **Gently sprinkle cocoa powder over the surface of the CD case.** Is cocoa powder going to work when you try this on a dark surface? What else could you use? What happens when you very gently brush the powder until the fingerprint appears?

- **Carefully place a piece of clear tape on top of the fingerprint and lift the print by gently peeling the tape off.** When you press the tape onto an index card, does the print pattern transfer to the card? Was it easy to lift the print? What can you do to make the print clearer?

To investigate more, try leaving a fingerprint on different surfaces like glass, plastic, wood, or granite. Which are the most visible? Are some surfaces easier to lift prints from than others? Also try baking soda, talcum powder, or flour to dust the prints. Does the type of powder affect your results?

Ideas for Supplies ▼

- clear CD case
- cocoa powder
- small paint or makeup brush
- clear tape
- white, unlined index cards
- magnifying glass

MATCH THE PRINT

Once forensic scientists have found, lifted, and examined a fingerprint, they try to match it against a print taken from a suspect or other known source. Now that you have learned how to look for the fingerprint patterns and characteristics that make each print unique, you can learn how to match two prints—just as forensic scientists do—to link a suspect to a crime scene.

FORENSIC CAREERS— FINGERPRINT EXAMINER

A fingerprint examiner is one type of forensic scientist. This key person in most crime labs compares fingerprints from crime scenes to prints from suspects and fingerprint databases. Fingerprint examiners may also visit the crime scene to find, photograph, and lift prints. Fingerprint examiners are skilled in using the various light and chemical processes for exposing latent prints and in following all of the procedures to properly protect and collect crime scene prints.

- **From your group of volunteers, secretly select one person to press his or her pointer finger onto an inkpad and leave a print on a white index card.** Keep this person's identity hidden from the group. Label the card as your crime scene print.

- **Using an inkpad, fingerprint your entire group of volunteer suspects.** Place each suspect's fingerprint on a separate white index card labeled with his or her name.

- **Using a magnifying glass, examine the fingerprint found at the crime scene.** What patterns and characteristics do you see?

- **What do you see when you compare the crime scene fingerprint against each fingerprint from your suspects?** Record your notes in a suspect log. Eliminate any prints that do not share the same basic pattern as your crime scene print. Look for minutiae points on the suspect prints that match the crime scene print. Can you make a preliminary conclusion that one suspect's print matches the print found at the crime scene? Which came the closest? How many points of similarity did you find?

> To investigate more, try matching a partial print to your suspect's fingerprints. Do you have enough information to make a positive match with just part of a print?

Ideas for Supplies

- several volunteers
- inkpad
- white index cards
- magnifying glass
- pencil
- paper

Ideas for
Supplies ▼

- clean glass
  jar with lid
- bottle cap
- super glue
- tweezers

I HOPE MY
FOREHEAD IS
GREASY ENOUGH...

LIFTING PRINTS—
CHEMICAL METHOD

One method of lifting prints uses a chemical found in super glue called cyanoacrylate. When heated, the chemicals in the glue evaporate into the air. When the evaporated glue encounters the residue that makes a fingerprint, it reacts to form a white material and a fingerprint appears.

Caution: Be very careful when handling super glue. Adult supervision is required.

- **Rub your finger over your forehead or the side of your nose to make it oily.** Press your finger somewhere on the inside of the glass, being careful not to smear or smudge your fingerprint.

- **Fill the bottle cap with super glue, making sure not to spill any on your fingers.** Using tweezers, carefully place the bottle cap in the jar and put the lid on tightly.

- **Let the jar sit in a warm place for about one hour.** Bring the jar outside where you can open it and allow the glue fumes to escape safely. Remove the lid carefully, without tipping the jar and spilling any remaining glue.

- **What do you see?** If you see fingerprints, what differences do you find between dusting for prints and chemical lifting?

To investigate more, have several people leave fingerprints inside the glass jar. After fuming to reveal the prints, try to match each print to its owner.

Chapter 3 ▶
Blood Evidence

When is a liquid
blood, and how
is blood used to
solve a crime?

>> To read blood's clues, a forensic specialist must understand the properties of blood and how it reacts to forces that act upon it.

As investigators arrive at a crime scene, they notice immediately that blood is scattered throughout the room. Blood spatter stains the wall, blood drops crisscross the floor, and a smeared print covers the door handle. There is no body. There are no witnesses. Did a crime occur here and, if so, what happened? Using blood evidence, investigators begin to piece together the events.

Bloodstains at a crime scene can reveal a great deal of information. The shape and location of bloodstains can show where a victim and assailant were during the crime and their movements at the scene. Bloodstain patterns can also reveal information about the crime. Did the blood drip from an open wound or did it spray from a punch to the face? Even more useful is that DNA from blood can identify a victim or suspect.

WHAT IS BLOOD?

Your arteries and veins pump blood throughout your body. Blood carries the oxygen and fuel your body needs, and transports waste products to the kidneys, lungs, and digestive system where they are removed from the body. Whole blood is a mixture of solid blood cells and liquid plasma. Plasma is a yellowish fluid that is 90 percent water and contains nutrients, proteins, and waste products. Within the plasma, solid red and white blood cells and platelets are suspended and carried along. These solids make blood thicker than water. Red blood cells contain a protein called hemoglobin that gives blood its bright red color.

While blood is moving through the body, it remains in a liquid state. When someone dies and their blood is no longer moving through the body, or when blood spills outside the body, it reacts like other liquids. It flows according to the force of gravity. Drops of blood flow to and collect at the lowest surface point.

HOW DOES BLOOD CLOT?

Within a few minutes of being outside the body, blood begins to clot. When blood clots, its solid components separate from liquid plasma, clumping together to form a dark red solid mass. When you cut yourself, clotting seals the cut with a scab. When spilled blood clots, it separates into dark-red solid clots and a clear yellow liquid called serum. Investigators use clotting to estimate how much time has passed since blood was spilled.

>> **An investigator can link a suspect to a crime scene if his or her blood is found at the scene or if the victim's blood is found on something in the suspect's possession.**

Blood is the most common body fluid left at a crime scene.

FORENSIC FACT

In a typical case, blood begins to clot within three to 15 minutes of leaving the body. When it begins to clot, blood forms a shiny, jelly-like substance. As more time passes, red clots separate from the yellow serum.

FORENSIC FACT

Years ago, police assumed that if it looked like blood at a crime scene, it probably was. But in 1967, the United States Supreme Court overturned a conviction because prosecutors had relied on red-stained shorts as proof of a crime. The red stains turned out to be paint, not blood. Since then, police and prosecutors have used scientific tests to confirm blood evidence.

If investigators find a pool of liquid blood at a crime scene, they can conclude that the blood was shed only a few minutes earlier. If the blood has become a shiny, gelatinous substance, clotting has begun and the investigators estimate that the bleeding took place within the past hour. When spilled blood has already separated into solid red clots and yellow serum, several hours may have passed since the blood spilled.

IS IT BLOOD?

A pool of blood around a dead body is easy to spot. Yet sometimes blood is more difficult to see, especially if a suspect has tried to clean it up before investigators arrive at the scene. Other times, it may not even look like blood. Old, dried blood, for example, can be mistaken for purple paint or brown grease stains. On the other hand, not every red substance at a crime scene is blood. Therefore, when investigators find a suspicious liquid or stain at a crime scene, they analyze three main questions:

1. Is it blood?

2. Is it human blood?

3. Whose blood is it?

Investigators use several tests at a crime scene to find blood. They can illuminate the crime scene with a high-intensity light or ultraviolet light that reveals traces of blood that are not easily seen under normal lights.

Investigators may also use presumptive tests to detect blood. Presumptive tests use a chemical that reacts with the hemoglobin in blood and fall into two basic categories. Some tests cause a color-change reaction when exposed to blood, and others cause a fluorescent or glowing reaction.

Using the Kastle-Meyer test, investigators collect a blood sample on a cotton swab and apply a clear solution of phenolphthalein and hydrogen peroxide to the sample. If blood is present, a chemical reaction with hemoglobin produces a pink solution.

Fluorescent tests make blood glow under ultraviolet light. Investigators spray a fluorescent chemical, such as Luminol, over a surface where they think there may be traces of blood. The area is darkened, and UV lights are turned on. Because Luminol is sensitive to the smallest traces of blood, it can detect blood that has been diluted up to 300,000 times.

While presumptive tests give quick results in the field, they are not 100 percent accurate. Sometimes other substances can cause a false positive result, causing the test to show that the sample is blood when it isn't. For this reason, any sample that tests positive for blood using a presumptive test is tested again in the crime lab to confirm it is blood.

Investigators carefully collect samples of any blood they find and take them back to the crime lab. At the lab, a forensic biologist called a serologist performs tests to determine if the sample is human or animal blood. Sometimes pets or other animals are at a crime scene and can be the source of a bloodstain.

WHOSE BLOOD IS IT?

Once forensic scientists confirm that a sample is human blood, the next step is to determine who shed the blood. A blood sample belonging to either a suspect or a victim is powerful evidence.

For many years, the first step in identifying a blood sample was determining its blood type. There are four human blood types: A, B, AB, and O. Certain proteins present in red blood cells determine your blood type.

DNA: The Key to Identity

Blood, hair, and other body substances found at a crime scene help identify a suspect or victim. Other than red blood cells, every cell in your body holds DNA. This is a long molecule found in the nucleus of cells in almost every living thing. DNA provides the information needed to create a living thing and keep it working. In each cell nucleus, the DNA molecule is in the shape of a twisted ladder called a double helix. At the end of each ladder rung are small molecules called bases. The order of the bases and DNA sequence for every person, animal, or plant is unique. Unless you have an identical twin, there is no one else on Earth who has the same DNA as you. Investigators can compare DNA found at a crime scene to DNA from a suspect. If it matches, the investigator has linked the suspect to the crime scene.

While a sample's blood type cannot specifically identify its source, it can rule out suspects. If a suspect has type A blood and the crime scene blood is type O, it is not the suspect's blood. But if the suspect's blood type matches the sample found at the scene, investigators will perform further tests. Today many forensic labs use DNA testing to compare DNA from the crime scene sample against DNA samples from the suspect. If DNA sections from the suspect and crime scene samples match, scientists have confirmed evidence that the blood belongs to the suspect.

Several factors affect DNA at a crime scene. Because heat, sunlight, moisture, bacteria, and mold can damage a DNA sample, not all DNA evidence will be useful in an investigation. If it is too damaged, scientists may not be able to use the sample as a match against a suspect's DNA. In addition, DNA found at a crime scene does not have a time stamp. While investigators may be able to link a suspect to the scene through DNA, they cannot say when the suspect was there or how long he or she spent at the scene.

BLOOD TELLS A STORY

Blood can leave the body in many ways. It can drip, ooze, flow, gush, or spurt. Each type of movement leaves a different and recognizable pattern. When investigators find bloodstains at a crime scene, they can use blood's physical properties to recreate what happened.

Blood doesn't just leave the body for no reason. It must be acted upon by a force. Sometimes, the force of gravity causes blood to separate from its source. Blood drips off an arm or a weapon and falls to the ground in a pool, leaving behind a passive bloodstain.

Sometimes a force is applied to the blood that causes a projected bloodstain. An assailant punches a victim's nose, for example, causing blood to spray across the wall. Bloodstains can also be created when a wet, bloody object comes in contact with another surface. Bloody fingerprints or shoe prints are examples of contact bloodstains. If a wet bloodstain is smeared or wiped when an object moves through it, a swipe pattern is left behind.

Investigators use blood pools, spatter, stains, and smears to understand the events at a crime scene. The shape, number, and pattern of bloodstains can help investigators answer questions like:

- **Where or who** did the blood come from?

- **What type of force** and/or weapon caused the bloodstain?

- **What was the distance** between the blood source and the stain?

- **What was the sequence** of events that led to the bloodstains?

- **What positions** were the victim, suspect, and witnesses in?

- **Is there evidence** of a struggle or was the assault one-sided?

- **Does the bloodstain pattern** support witness and suspect statements about the events at the scene?

SPATTER SIZE AND SHAPE

Blood spatter is a collection of blood spots that may be different sizes and shapes. Spatters are created when blood is acted upon by a force. Something causes the blood to travel through the air and land on a surface.

>> **Sections of DNA can actually be pulled out of blood cells.**

FORENSIC FACT

The Combined DNA Index System (CODIS) is an electronic database of DNA profiles that can identify suspects. CODIS contains DNA profiles from people convicted of crimes such as rape, murder, and child abuse. Investigators can search for a match in CODIS for an unknown DNA sample at a crime scene.

>> **Just by examining the size and shape of blood spatter, investigators can gather all sorts of useful information.**

WAS THE VICTIM STANDING?

FROM THE POOLING, HE WAS PROBABLY ON HIS KNEES...

When blood drips, gravity pulls it down toward the earth. As it falls through the air, a drop of blood has a spherical shape. It remains in a spherical shape until it hits a surface or another object. Then it splashes in a circular pattern around the point of impact.

As a blood drop falls, it gains speed. The greater the speed, the more the drop spatters on impact. This affects both the diameter of the stain and what the edges of the blood spatter look like. A slowly moving drop will have smooth, round edges. A faster-moving drop will have more scalloped edges with a series of continuous curves. If a drop moves fast enough, it may even bounce off the surface and splash back down, making a ring of smaller drops around the edge of the first spatter.

The type of surface a blood drop hits also affects its shape. When blood hits a hard, smooth, nonporous surface like glass, tile, or marble, it creates smaller spatter and has smooth, round edges. A rough, porous surface such as unfinished wood or concrete creates larger spatter with jagged edges.

Investigators can calculate the angle at which blood hit the surface from the shape of blood spatter. Blood that hits at an exact 90-degree angle will form an even circle around the point of impact. If the blood hits a surface at a different angle, however, the edge that strikes first will be round, while the far side will be irregular. This causes the spatter to have an elongated oval shape with the narrow end pointing in the drop's direction of travel. The steeper the angle, the more elongated the blood drop will be. Investigators can use lasers to follow the angle of impact from several stains. The point where the lasers converge can identify where the victim and assailant stood at the crime scene.

VELOCITY AND FORCE

Blood spatter can be classified by velocity or the force applied to it. Passive or low-velocity spatter falls solely due to gravity. This type of spatter usually comes from an open wound or drips from an object covered in blood. These spatters are generally large and circular in shape. The size of the spatter is determined by the height from which the blood falls. The higher the fall, the larger the diameter of the resulting shape.

Spatter created by a medium amount of force or at medium velocity is produced by gravity combined with some other force. Projected spatter will break into smaller-size shapes on impact. This type of pattern is usually seen when someone is hit with a blunt object or is stabbed. A high-velocity force can result in tiny droplets of spatter. A strong force causes the blood droplets to break into a large number of tiny pieces, producing a fog or mist of blood. Gunshots, explosions, and high-speed collisions can cause this type of blood spatter.

A COMPLICATED SCENE

Even with all the clues that bloodstains reveal, interpreting blood evidence at a crime scene can be extremely complicated. There may be overlapping blood spatter from multiple wounds or victims that makes it hard to recreate the crime. Blood spatter is delicate and can be destroyed or damaged by the victim, suspect, witnesses, investigators, or anyone else who moves through the crime scene. That is why blood spatter is carefully photographed using a grid to preserve the spatter patterns. These photographic images can be used later in crime scene reconstruction.

≫ Investigators measure the elongated spatter to calculate the angle at which the blood struck the surface.

FORENSIC FACT

Sometimes the absence of blood can be a clue. When investigators can't find a blood spatter in an area where they would expect to find one, they may decide that the attacker or another person at the scene was standing in that spot, blocking the blood spatter and thus leaving an empty space where blood spatter should have been.

BLOOD OR NOT?

Blood can look like many different substances, especially if the sample is small, dried, smeared, or mixed with another substance. Forensic scientists often use Hemastix to perform a simple and quick screening test in the field to determine whether a sample is or is not blood. If the test comes back positive, the evidence is sent to the crime lab where scientists analyze blood and DNA samples. If a sample turns out not to be blood, more detailed tests are needed to reveal the identity of the substance.

You can test for the presence of blood using Hemastix. These plastic strips detect hemoglobin in a substance. Hemastix are not hard to find. Pick some up at your local drugstore and you can test samples for blood.

Caution: Adult supervision is required when using bleach.

- **How many different liquid substances can you find to test for blood?** Gather your samples and place them on paper plates or in small bowls.

- **Which substances do you think will test positive or negative for blood?** Create a chart to record your predictions and observations for each substance. Record your predictions on your chart.

- **Dip a cotton swab into the first substance you want to test.** Press the swab against the indicator end of the Hemastix for a few seconds. Observe and record the color change. Do the same for each of your samples.

- **Which substances tested positive? Which tested negative?** Compare your results against your predictions. Did any tests result in a false positive? Why do you think that happened?

To investigate more, dilute the blood in water or another liquid. Does the Hemastix still register the presence of blood? Gradually increase the dilution of blood and retest. At what dilution does the test stop registering the presence of blood? What happens if you let the substance dry out first? If you swipe a damp cotton swab on a dried blood stain, does the Hemastix test positive for blood?

Ideas for Supplies ▼

- Substances to test, including blood from a package of meat or blood-soaked plastic pad from underneath meat, ketchup, bleach, red food coloring
- several paper plates or small bowls
- paper and pencil
- cotton swabs
- Hemastix (found online or at your local drug store)

BLOOD SPATTER PATTERNS

Blood spatter is a collection of blood spots, which may be different sizes and shapes depending on how they were formed. Blood spatter differs depending on the amount of blood, the speed of the drop, the angle at which it hits the ground, and the distance the drop travels.

- **Create some fake blood by mixing ¼ cup white corn syrup and 4–6 drops of red food coloring.** Use it to distinguish different spatter shapes and surfaces. You're going to want to cover a hard, flat surface with newspaper as this experiment can get messy. Then place a piece of white paper over that.

- **A chart will help you keep track of your data.** You will want to record the diameter of blood spatter, the shape, the height from which a sample dropped, and the angle.

- **Fill the dropper with fake blood. Release one drop of blood from exactly 1 foot above the paper (30.5 centimeters).** Release more drops of blood onto the paper from various heights and label each drop. Examine the edges of each drop with a magnifying glass. Do you notice any differences based on the height from which the drops fell? Record your measurements and observations.

- **Measure the diameter of each drop.** Use graph paper to create a scatter plot of your data for height and diameter. What does this graph with just the data points look like? What pattern or relationship do you observe between height and the diameter of the drops? How could you use this relationship to predict height from blood spatter found at a crime scene?

- **Try creating blood drops that hit at different angles.** Can you think of ways to make the drops hit the surface at an angle? Use a magnifying glass to examine each drop, noting size, shape, and edges. How do the angled drops differ from drops that fell straight down?

To investigate more, repeat the experiment using different surfaces. What happens on rough surfaces like concrete or asphalt? What about a smooth surface such as tile? What differences do you observe? Can you think of ways to make blood drops hit surfaces with more than just the force of gravity? What happens when you squirt blood across a surface? Experiment with different methods and different amounts of blood. You might need to make a lot more fake blood for this.

Ideas for Supplies

- fake blood
- newspaper
- white paper
- notebook paper
- dropper
- yardstick
- ruler
- magnifying glass
- graph paper

Chapter 4 ▶
Bones and Bodies

What story can bones
tell about what
happened to a body?

I THINK WE FOUND SOMETHING OVER HERE.

LOOKS LIKE WE NEED SOME HELP.

YES, WE NEED A FORENSIC ANTHROPOLOGIST OUT HERE.

WE NEED PHOTOS.

>> When a corpse is examined in an autopsy, forensic pathologists examine every inch of the body, inside and out.

FORENSIC FACT

Everyone has the same basic skeleton. There are 206 bones in the normal human adult body. Bones support our bodies and provide a place for muscles to attach. Bone joints allow us to move our arms and legs. Bones also protect the body's internal organs, particularly the brain, spinal cord, heart, and lungs.

A body at a crime scene can hold many clues for investigators. Maybe a victim carries a wallet with identification in his or her pocket. Or investigators can identify the victim by matching fingerprints or dental records. They look for evidence and clues that reveal how and when the victim died, and the sequence of events that led to his or her death.

BONES: A PIECE OF THE PUZZLE

In some cases, a complete body is not found. A crime team may have as little as a single bone to examine. When a forensic anthropologist comes in to examine bones, he or she tries to answer several questions with the forensic pathologist:

1. Are the bones human?

2. To whom do they belong?

3. How long has the victim been dead?

4. What is the cause of death and manner of death?

Although we all have the same types of bones in our bodies, there are variations in the bones of different groups of people. Forensic anthropologists use these variations to learn more about the victim's identity. They use bumps, grooves, indentations, overall size, thickness, and other bone characteristics to develop a profile of the victim. With a full, intact adult skeleton, a forensic anthropologist can estimate the victim's gender, age within 5 to 10 years, and height to within 1 or 2 inches (2.5 to 5 centimeters). They can also uncover clues about recent injuries, cause of death, other aspects of the past history of the victim, and possibly retrieve DNA samples from the bones and teeth. But time and nature sometimes take their toll by scattering or destroying many pieces of a skeleton, leaving investigators with little to examine.

IS IT A HUMAN OR AN ANIMAL?

To the untrained eye, many animal bones look like human bones. The bones from a bear's front paw can easily be mistaken for a human hand. Sheep and deer have ribs that are similar to human ribs. Yet because each vertebrate species has evolved differently, human and animal bones have different internal structures, densities, and shapes. Forensic anthropologists are trained to analyze these distinctions to determine if bones found at a crime scene are human or animal.

FORENSIC CAREERS: FORENSIC PATHOLOGIST

A forensic pathologist examines bodies to determine the cause and manner of death. To find answers, the forensic pathologist performs autopsies, runs the pathology lab, examines the crime scene, and helps law enforcement with finding and preserving human remains. A forensic pathologist may be a medical examiner or work in the medical examiner or coroner's offices. They have a medical license and have studied anatomy, pathology, anthropology, and dentistry. They also need to understand evidence rules, crime scene and court procedures, and federal, state, and local laws.

HOW OLD WAS THE VICTIM?

Bones can hold several clues to a victim's age. In children and teens, teeth and bones grow and develop at a predictable rate. While a child is still growing, the ends of the long bones are mostly cartilage. As bone shafts lengthen and bone gradually replaces cartilage, a layer of cartilage called the growth plate separates the end of each bone from the bone shaft. Between the ages of 17 and 25, most teenagers and young adults stop growing and the development of their bones is complete. By assessing the stage of bone development and measuring bone length, forensic anthropologists can estimate a narrow range for the victim's age.

For young people up to age 21, teeth are the most accurate sign of age because teeth follow a regular pattern of growth and development. Most children have lost their baby teeth and have their permanent adult teeth by age 12. Most teens have their wisdom teeth by age 18.

Even bones in fully grown adults offer insight into a victim's age. As people age, the surface of some bones change, including the skull, pubic bones, and ribs. Throughout a person's life, bones make new osteons, which are tiny tubes that hold blood vessels. Examining the cross-section of a bone under a microscope allows investigators to see the tubes. Younger adults have fewer and larger osteons, while older adults have more, smaller osteons. On the ribs, the areas where the bone meets the breastbone are smooth and rounded in a young person, but become pitted and sharper as a person ages. As we age, our bones lose density and calcium. X-rays provide a look at these elements of bone decay.

HEIGHT AND BUILD

Forensic anthropologists can draw a picture of a person's body type by examining bones to estimate height. There is a correlation between a person's height and the length of several bones in the legs and arms, including the tibia, fibula, and humerus. If any of these bones is found at the crime scene, a forensic anthropologist will measure it and calculate a height estimate for the victim.

In addition, the diameter of bones can tell a forensic anthropologist about the victim's build. If bones are thick, the person probably had a more muscular build, while a slight person usually has thinner bones.

MALE OR FEMALE?

How do forensic anthropologists determine if a skeleton is male or female? To begin, the overall size and sturdiness of the bones can give a clue. Males tend to have larger, thicker bones and bone joints. They also tend to have more bone development where muscles attach. The thickness of specific regions of certain bones may be larger in men than in women. For example, the diameter of the head of the humerus, radius, and femur are generally larger in men than women.

The pelvic bones, if available, are some of the most accurate to determine if a skeleton is male or female. During puberty, a female's pelvic bones adapt for childbirth. They become wider to allow a baby to pass through, and the sciatic notch becomes wider too. In women who have already delivered a child, the backside of the pubic bone may be scarred or indicate other damage from childbirth.

FORENSIC CAREERS: FORENSIC ANTHROPOLOGIST

When bones or a body is found, investigators call a forensic anthropologist. The forensic anthropologist assists the medical examiner in collecting the bones and other remains from the crime scene. At the lab, they clean the bones and examine them closely. A forensic anthropologist works with the medical examiner or coroner to estimate the victim's biological profile (age, gender, height, race, and other details). Forensic anthropologists may visit burial sites and help remove bodies and other human remains. They examine tissue, bones, and other remains to help identify people.

>> Kids develop at their own pace, so it is not perfect science. But looking at a victim's teeth can help a forensic anthropologist come up with a reasonable estimated age.

>> A victim's teeth may be the most useful part of the entire skeleton for identification. Teeth can be matched to a person's individual dental records, which contain a description of every tooth and any dental work that has been done.

FORENSIC FACT

Paul Revere was a dentist. During the Revolutionary War he used teeth to help identify the dead.

ANCESTRY

Determining a victim's race or ancestry from his or her bones can be very difficult. There is no single skeletal trait that is specific to any one group. Instead, forensic anthropologists study bone characteristics, particularly the skull, for clues that may reveal a victim's ancestry. The skull's bones have inherited features that are passed down from one generation to the next. By identifying these features and comparing them to data from world populations, a forensic anthropologist can make an educated guess as to the victim's an ancestry.

People of European ancestry tend to have high rounded or square skulls. They have straighter and narrower faces with narrow, protruding nasal bones. People with sub-Saharan African ancestry generally have lower, narrower skulls, wider-set eye sockets, and wider, flatter nasal bones. Those with Asian ancestry tend to have skulls that are broader and flatter around the face, with forward-sloping cheekbones, lower nasal bones, and round eye sockets. Studying and measuring a skull and comparing the skull against known characteristics can help a forensic anthropologist determine the ancestry of the victim.

TEETH

Forensic odontologists are specially trained dentists who use teeth and bite marks or dental impressions to identify a specific person. Like fingerprints, we all have a unique set of teeth. The odontologist uses the alignment of the teeth, fillings, and any other characteristics to match a set of impressions or teeth to a suspect or victim.

X-rays identify hidden details such as caps, crowns, and root canals, which can be useful for identification. Special scanning electron microscopes and computer modeling programs allow investigators to match bite marks on a victim's body to a mold of a suspect's teeth.

CLUES TO THE CRIME

Bones can also reveal clues about the cause and manner of death. Cause of death is the specific reason a person died, such as a heart attack or drowning. The manner of death is the root cause that leads to the sequence of events that ended the victim's life. The manner of death includes how and why a victim died. Was death caused by the victim, another person, an accident, or natural causes? Manner of death also considers who or what started the chain of events that led to the victim's death.

A bone with fractures, fragmentation, or impact marks may indicate that the victim was hit with a blunt object. Cut surfaces on the bone can mean the victim was struck with an ax or knife. Gunshots leave recognizable entry and exit wounds and gouges on bones and skulls.

In addition to determining what caused the bone injury, the forensic anthropologist can also determine if the injury was related to the victim's death or if it was a previous, unrelated injury. When a person is alive, bone injuries and fractures heal after the initial injury. Fractured bones that are healing show callus or scar formation. If a forensic anthropologist finds signs of healing around a bone injury, he or she can reasonably conclude that the injury did not occur near the time of death.

ESTIMATING TIME OF DEATH

When a body is found at a crime scene, forensic investigators examine it to estimate when the death occurred. Knowing when a victim died can eliminate a suspect with an alibi for the time of death. For example, a medical examiner may estimate a woman was killed between 8 and 10 pm. If several people confirm that her husband was at a dinner party during that time, it is unlikely that he killed her. A suspect without an alibi for the time of death may have to answer more questions.

If a body is found soon after death, a medical examiner can use body temperature to estimate time of death. A live body is approximately 98.6 degrees Fahrenheit (37 degrees Celsius). The body's temperature drops at a rate of about 1.5 degrees per hour after death, until it reaches the temperature of its surroundings. The cooling of the body after death is called algor mortis. The rate of cooling can vary based on the surrounding conditions. For example, a body in a warm room will lose heat more slowly than a body in a cold barn. Other factors, such as obesity, clothing, exposure to sunlight, and an enclosed environment can slow heat loss.

After death, chemical reactions cause the body's muscles to contract and become stiff, a condition called rigor mortis. The stiffening happens at predictable rates, which allows investigators to use rigor mortis to estimate time of death. Under normal conditions, rigor mortis sets in about two hours after death. It begins in the small muscles of the face and moves downward from head to toe to larger muscles. Complete rigor mortis, when the entire body is rigid, takes about 8 to 12 hours. The body remains that way for another 18 hours, before the process begins to reverse. Therefore, rigor mortis can only be used for about 36 to 48 hours after death to estimate time of death. It is also one of the least reliable methods to estimate time of death because its progress varies a lot with the temperature of the environment. Rigor mortis speeds up in hotter environments, and slows in colder environments.

If a body is not found a few hours after death, a medical examiner can look at where the flesh and bones of a body are in the decomposition process to estimate an approximate time of death. The intestines, which hold many bacteria, decay first, followed by the liver, lungs, brain, and kidneys. Decomposition of the stomach may be slower because it holds food and acids that slow bacteria.

Obesity, clothing, and temperature can speed up or slow down both processes of decomposition, as can the location of the body. Typically, a body that is exposed to the environment will decay faster than one that is buried, frozen, or under water. Insects can also speed up the rate of decomposition, until only a skeleton remains.

>> The decomposition of the body involves two processes. The first process, called autolysis, occurs as the enzymes in the cells chemically break down the body's cells and tissues. The second process, called putrefaction, occurs when bacteria destroy the body's tissues.

FORENSIC FACT

At the University of Tennessee Medical Center, a research facility called the Body Farm has a field of dead bodies where researchers study decomposition. By studying the decomposition of human bodies, they can better understand how decomposition works and how it can be used to solve crimes.

USING BONES TO PREDICT HEIGHT

Forensic anthropologists often do not have an intact body or skeleton to examine. Instead, these scientists can build a picture of the victim with only a few bones as clues. The tibia, the inner leg bone that joins the knee to the ankle, is one bone that forensic anthropologists use to predict the height of a victim.

- **By measuring several volunteers, you will see the correlation between height and bones and understand how scientists use bones to predict height.** Create a chart to record all measurements, keeping your data separate for males and females. Carefully measure and record each volunteer's height in centimeters. Then measure and record the length of the tibia bone in centimeters by determining the distance from just below the kneecap to the ankle.

- several volunteers (at least 10 of each gender)
- paper and pencil
- metric tape measure
- graph paper
- second group of volunteers

- **Now divide the height by the tibia length to get a decimal number that represents the ratio of height to tibia length.** Can you calculate the average of your ratios? Plot the ratios on a graph, making one for males and one for females. Does your graph have a shape? Does it look like a bell curve with the average at the highest point of the bell and outliers in lower numbers to the right or left of the curve?

- **Create a formula to predict height from the length of a tibia bone.** Use the average ratio you discovered in your investigation. For example, if the average ratio from your graph was 4:1, that would mean that the average person is four times as tall as his tibia bone.

- **Now test your own formula by gathering tibia measurements from another group of volunteers.** Then using your formula, predict their height from the tibia measurements. Compare your predictions against the actual heights. How accurate are your formula and predictions? How could you adjust your formula to make your predictions more accurate?

To investigate more, repeat the experiment with the humerus bone. Investigators also use this upper arm bone that reaches from the elbow to the shoulder to predict height. Is the tibia or humerus bone a more accurate predictor of height?

I WONDER IF IT'S TRUE FOR ALL SKELETONS?

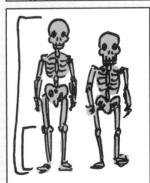

EXTRACT YOUR OWN DNA

Every person's DNA is different. DNA collected from a crime scene can link a suspect to the evidence, placing a person at a crime scene, in a car, in a room, or in a house even if they claim not to have been there. On the other hand, when a DNA sample does not match a suspect's DNA, it can support the suspect's statement that he or she was never there. DNA can be found in saliva, blood, hair follicles, and other bodily fluids or tissues left at a crime scene. When investigators have a suspect, they often obtain a DNA sample and compare it to the DNA evidence at the scene.

You can extract some of your own DNA and see what it looks like even without using a microscope.

Caution: This activity uses ethyl alcohol, which is highly flammable. Do not do this experiment anywhere near an open flame or a gas stove! Adult supervision is required.

- **You'll need to have a couple of solutions on hand.** First, create a 25 percent soap solution by mixing one part shampoo with three parts water in a paper cup. 1 tablespoon of shampoo should be enough. Put the soap solution aside.

- **Have an empty paper cup nearby.** Swish a little of the sports drink around in your mouth for at least 30 seconds and spit it into the cup. Cells from your saliva and the inside of your cheek are now dissolved in the sports drink.

- **Pour some of the sports drink into the test tube, leaving enough room to add about 2 milliliters of the soap solution.** Add the soap solution and gently swirl the liquids together in the test tube. If you swirl the mixture too hard, you'll break up the DNA, so be careful. Let it sit for two minutes.

- **Measure 3 milliliters of ethyl alcohol in an eyedropper.** Holding the test tube at an angle, slowly release the ethyl alcohol along the side of the tube until you see a layer form on top of the soap solution. Why do you think the alcohol stays on top?

- **Wait 2 minutes before examining the contents of the test tube.** Do you see any small dots or strands floating in the ethyl alcohol? These are clumps of your tangled DNA molecules! The salt from the sports drink helps the DNA stick together. If you want to keep your DNA, use a wooden stick or a straw to collect the strands and transfer them to a small container filled with alcohol.

To investigate more, try using different soaps and detergents. How do powdered soaps work compared to liquid detergents? What about shampoo or liquid body soap? Try experimenting with other sources of DNA, such as strawberries or peas. You can blend ½ cup (100 milliliters) of these foods up raw with ⅛ teaspoon of salt (less than 1 milliliter) and 1 cup of cold water (200 milliliters) to replace your saliva and sports drink solution.

Ideas for Supplies

- shampoo
- water
- paper cups
- clear sports drink
- large test tube with cap
- 95% ethyl alcohol
- graduated cylinder with milliliter markings
- eye dropper

THE SUSPECT'S DNA IS NOT A MATCH TO WHAT WAS FOUND AT THE CRIME SCENE.

MATCH THE BITE MARK

Like fingerprints, teeth marks can be used to identify suspects and victims. A forensic odontologist uses dentistry to identify bite marks and human remains. Each person has a unique set of teeth. How the teeth are aligned, and if there are any fillings or chipped teeth, are some details that help a forensic odontologist match teeth or bite marks to a suspect.

Using Styrofoam plates, you can collect dental impressions from volunteers and see if you can identify the crime scene bite!

- **Each of your volunteers is going to bite a Styrofoam plate.** You might want to demonstrate how to leave a bite mark impression on the plate. Fold a plate in half carefully so you don't break it. Put the center of the folded plate into your mouth as far as possible and bite down on it to make a good impression. Just don't bite so deeply that you go through the plate.

- **Have your volunteers make their impressions and write their names on their plates, labeling the maxilla (top jaw) and mandible (bottom jaw).** Make a chart and write down the width and depth of the maxilla and mandible for each volunteer. Also note any unique characteristics that might help you identify the suspect.

- **While you're out of the room, have one volunteer make a crime scene bite mark impression on a Styrofoam plate.** It should be cut into a square. The volunteers should not tell you who did it.

- **Time to test your odontology skills.** Compare the teeth impressions from the crime scene bite mark to the impressions collected from your volunteer suspects. What unique characteristics can you see? Can you identify which suspect made the crime scene bite mark? Which characteristics of the teeth impressions were most useful when comparing the different sets of bite marks? Is there any other information that would have been useful to collect?

> To investigate more, ask people who have dental work such as braces, expanders, or pulled teeth to leave bite marks to see if these bites are easier to identify.

Ideas for Supplies ▼

- Styrofoam plates
- scissors
- several volunteers
- pen
- ruler or measuring tape

Chapter 5

Making an Impression: Marks and Prints

Can footprints, tire tracks, and tool marks identify a specific suspect?

>> Identifying the type of shoe can narrow down the suspect list and eliminate some people, but does not specifically identify or link a specific person to the crime scene.

Although a criminal may have long since fled the scene, a mark left behind can put investigators on his trail. Shoes, tools, and tires all leave marks and impressions that forensic scientists can use to track down a suspect.

When an object presses against another material and leaves an imprint, it creates an impression. Shoeprints, tool marks, tire tracks, and bite marks are all examples of impression evidence. Impressions may be formed in many different surfaces. Soil, mud, dust, concrete, wood, grass, and even skin can hold an impression. How clear the impression is depends on the object that makes the impression, as well as how hard or soft the surface is.

Impressions are usually class evidence. Class characteristics include things like size, manufacturer, and pattern design. Class evidence can exclude a suspect, but does not necessarily connect an individual suspect to a crime scene.

An investigator may be able to identify what type of shoe made a print, but thousands of people could have that same brand and size of shoe. For this reason, investigators look for individual evidence, or unique characteristics and wear patterns in the print or impression that will link it directly to the suspect.

FOOTPRINTS LEAVE A TRAIL

A footprint may not look like much, but investigators can use it to build a profile of a suspect. By studying a print and its shape, texture, and pattern, investigators can determine what type of shoe left the print. Identifying the type of shoe helps investigators learn about the person who made the print. A person who wears a work boot is probably very different from someone who wears a dance shoe. Whether a shoe is a newer, expensive shoe or an older, worn shoe may reveal relevant information about a suspect. Investigators use a footprint to make educated guesses about a suspect's gender, age, and activities. A footprint can also be used to estimate a suspect's height and weight. A small, shallow print is usually made by a short, light person, while a tall, heavy person leaves a large, deep print.

Footprints can reveal details about the events at the crime scene. A footprint made by a person walking is different from one made by the same person running or carrying a heavy object. Someone who is running usually leaves an impression that is deeper at the heel and toe. A person carrying a heavy object will make a deeper print overall than a person who is not carrying anything.

Theodore Kaczynski, also known as the Unabomber, attached smaller soles to the bottom of his shoes to confuse investigators.

FORENSIC FACT

If enough individualizing characteristics are present, just a 1-square-inch area of a shoeprint can be enough to positively identify it as having been made by the suspect's shoe.

Footprints found at a crime scene are placed into one of two categories. Positive prints are two-dimensional marks left by a dirty shoe on a hard surface. A person may have stepped in a substance such as oil, mud, dust, or blood and then left residue on the surface. Other times, a suspect will leave a three-dimensional depression when he or she steps on a soft surface such as dust, mud, or snow. This type of impression is called a negative footprint.

FORENSIC FACT

Casting shoeprints in snow can be quite difficult because snow tends to melt during the casting process. It is important that the investigator has a lot of experience using the materials that are available for this purpose, such as Snow Print Wax or melted sulfur.

The space between prints can be measured to estimate the suspect's stride. A shorter stride may suggest that the suspect was carrying something, while a longer stride may suggest the suspect was running when he or she left the print.

Footprints can also reveal points of entry and exit and movement at the crime scene. Investigators follow footprints in case the prints lead them to new pieces of evidence. Maybe the trail ends at a bullet casing or a discarded bag. Multiple shoeprints can show that more than one person was present at the crime scene. In addition, if the same shoeprint is found at multiple crime scenes, it may link a single suspect to several crimes.

Once a footprint is found, investigators photograph the print from several angles, often placing a ruler next to the print in the picture to document the print's size. Footprints left on dusty or oily surfaces can be lifted like fingerprints. For negative prints, investigators can fill the print's depression with plaster or dental stone to create a cast. Once hardened, the cast becomes a three-dimensional model and is sent to the forensic lab for further analysis. While at the crime scene, CSIs may also take shoe prints from the police and investigators at the scene to use as control samples.

At the crime lab, forensic scientists examine the print. They study its shape, size, pattern, and texture. To link a suspect to the crime scene, forensic scientists try to match the shoeprint to a specific shoe worn by the suspect. To do this, they first have to identify the type of shoe that left the print. Was it a running shoe? If so, what brand and model was it? To find out, investigators compare the print visually with other known prints. They compare the general outsole patterns and shapes, design features, and markings to identify the make, model, and size of the shoeprint.

Once investigators know the make and model, is there anything that makes the shoe unique? Every shoe has a few characteristics that are particular to its wearer. People wear the soles of their shoes in a distinct wear pattern. Some people walk on the outside of the foot, some shuffle, and others walk on the balls of the feet. How people walk and where they place pressure on the shoe affects how the sole of the shoe wears down.

The type of surfaces a person regularly walks on also affects a shoe's wear pattern. An office worker who walks across polished tile floors each day, for example, will have a different wear pattern on his or her shoes than a construction worker who is always walking across gravel and rough concrete surfaces. In addition, cuts, nicks, scratches, and gouges in the sole can make a shoeprint distinct.

TIRE TRACKS

Like shoes, the tires of cars, bikes, and motorcycles can leave tracks at a crime scene. When a tire rolls through mud, paint, blood, grime, or other materials, it picks up the material and transfers a visible print onto the road surface. Tires may also travel over soft ground, leaving a three-dimensional track. Sometimes a tire track is latent, or not visible to the naked eye, but can be seen with special lighting and technology.

To collect tire tracks, investigators first photograph the prints. Taking the picture from a 90-degree angle prevents distortions in the image. The investigator may lay a ruler next to the track to provide a size reference for the picture. Three-dimensional tracks are photographed, casted, and transported to the forensic lab.

》Taken together, a shoe's wear patterns and other distinctive marks can make a shoeprint as unique as a fingerprint. It can provide a piece of individual evidence pointing to a single suspect.

FORENSIC FACT

Some shoe manufacturers, especially the larger ones like Nike and Reebok, have people who assist law enforcement agencies to provide them with specific information. How many of a certain size were manufactured in a particular type or model of shoe, and where they were distributed, can be useful information for investigators.

>> Investigators measure tire tracks to calculate a vehicle's track width, wheelbase, and turning radius. This information narrows the possible car models that could have made the track.

FORENSIC FACT

The FBI, as well as a number of private companies, maintain shoeprint databases. These databases are updated regularly and include tens of thousands of images of the soles and the uppers of sports, work, and casual shoes. One of these private companies also has a tire tread database with over 5,000 images.

Investigators look at a tire's tread pattern to identify its size and manufacturer. Most tires have two to three rows of treads, called ribs. Between the ribs are channels, called grooves. The pattern of a tire's ribs and grooves varies by make, model, and manufacturer. To identify the type of tire, investigators compare the print to thousands of tire tracks stored in a tire tread database.

Once they have narrowed the search, forensic scientists study the tire tracks for distinctive marks and wear patterns that make the tire unique. Like shoes, tires wear in specific patterns that vary from tire to tire and car to car. Because the tires on a car may not be properly balanced or aligned, the wear on a tire may be different than it is on another tire from the same car. In addition, as tires travel over the road, they may collect cuts, tears, or debris. These details make a tire unique and can link it to a specific vehicle.

To compare a tire track to a suspect's tires, forensic scientists ink the suspect's tire and roll it down a long piece of paper. Then they compare the prints to those found at the crime scene. If they can match the prints using unique characteristics and wear patterns, they can link the suspect to the crime scene.

TOOL MARKS

A tool used at a crime scene can also leave behind a mark for forensic scientists to analyze for information. For example, if a suspect broke into a room, investigators may find screwdriver impressions in the paint along a doorframe.

A tool may also leave marks when it slides across or scratches a surface. These marks can leave a pattern of ridges or striations in the surface that can be used to narrow down the type of tool used. Tools that slice through materials, such as wire cutters, can leave cut marks with lines and striations that may be unique to those tools.

Individual manufacturing defects or use patterns on a tool can be used to match evidence at a crime scene to a tool in a suspect's possession. Two identical tools made by the same manufacturer may have tiny variations that make each unique and identifiable. As with most types of evidence, investigators photograph tool marks they find at a crime scene. Investigators may remove the object with the mark, such as a door or window frame, and send it to the lab. If the object cannot be moved, or if it cannot be moved carefully enough that the print won't be disturbed, investigators make a casting of the mark.

Forensic scientists study the tool marks using a microscope to see the smallest details. They analyze the ridges or striation patterns and look for any defects. To match the marks to a suspect's tool, the scientist will try to recreate the mark using the suspect's tool. They can then compare the marks found at the crime scene with the marks made by the suspect's tool. Many forensic labs use comparison microscopes that allow scientists to view two samples simultaneously. This way, they can make side-by-side comparisons of the two marks. If they can match the two, they can link the suspect to the crime scene.

>> A tool makes an impression or indentation mark when it strikes a soft surface such as putty, caulking, or thick paint, leaving details of the tool's shape and any imperfections on its surface.

TIRE TRACKS

To avoid being caught, criminals often speed away from a crime scene. While some run on foot, others jump into a waiting car or other vehicle to make a quick getaway. Fortunately for investigators, tires leave marks and prints that can help identify the vehicle used and create a trail leading to the suspect.

You can compare tire tracks made from different types of bicycles to learn how investigators identify and match tire prints at the crime scene.

- To make a surface that will leave an imprint, place a piece of carbon paper between two pieces of white paper. You will need a white paper–carbon paper stack for each tire you plan to print. Can you figure out how to keep the pieces from moving or shifting during the experiment?

- Find a flat surface to ride your bikes over. Lay a paper stack on the surface, making sure the carbon side is facing up, and make an imprint. Where should you place the paper stack so you can get a print of the back tire? On each piece of white paper with a tire print, label which bike and which tire made the print. Do this for each bike you are testing.

- Examine each tire print. Create a chart to record your observations. What details will be helpful? Some ideas might be the width and pattern of the tread. What other characteristics can you look at to distinguish one tire from another? Include them in your chart.

- Have a volunteer choose one bike and create another tire print without telling you which bike made the print. To make a full print of the whole tire, tape together several paper stacks. Compare the unidentified print with the labeled prints. Can you identify which bike made the print?

> To investigate more, have several volunteers of different weights make tire prints using the same bicycle. Are there any differences in the prints? You may also try changing the surface on which the print is made. How does this affect the print?

- several sheets of white paper
- several sheets of carbon paper
- tape
- several bicycles
- ruler
- magnifying glass

I WANT TO COLLECT ALL MY FRIENDS' TIRE TRACKS.

SHOE PRINT IMPRESSIONS

Sometimes a criminal will leave a shoeprint behind as he or she flees the crime scene. Some prints are left as an impression in a soft surface such as mud. These prints can help investigators identify a suspect. Investigators carefully photograph and cast the print, so that forensic scientists can examine it to determine the make, style, and size of the shoe. Scientists can also use the print to estimate the weight, height, and stride of the suspect. To make a cast of a depression shoe print, investigators fill the depression with plaster or dental stone. When the cast hardens, they carefully remove it and send it to the forensic lab.

Using an old shoe and some plaster of Paris, make your own impression in dirt and try casting it. You'll see how tricky it can be to get a cast that includes enough details to identify a print. It takes careful work! This can get messy, so you may want to do this experiment outside.

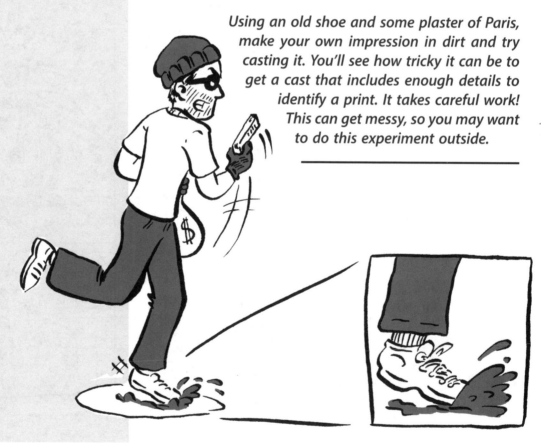

- **Use a contained space like a shoebox or plastic tub to make your impression.** Mix dirt and water to a consistency that you think will leave the clearest print. What will happen if it's too muddy or too dry? Do you want it smooth or clumpy? When your mud is ready, fill the container about 1 to 2 inches deep (2.5 to 5 centimeters).

- **Make a print with your full weight on the shoe so it leaves a clear impression.** Be careful not to disturb your print when you remove your shoe. It can help to spray the print with a fine mist of hair spray to hold the impression during casting. Are you satisfied with the print you made? You can always try again if you think you need more details.

- **Prepare the plaster of Paris in a paper cup.** When you pour it over the print, start from the side so it slowly fills into the impression. Pouring the plaster directly onto the depression can damage some of its markings. Let the cast sit and harden for 20 minutes to an hour before you remove it. Place it in a safe place to dry overnight. What did you notice about the casting process? Was it difficult to fill the print evenly with the plaster? What about removing the cast?

- **The next day, brush off any sand or dirt that may have stuck to the cast and examine the print.** What details help you identify the shoe's style and manufacturer? If you show your cast to a family member, can he or she identify the shoe it came from?

> To investigate more, prepare another container of dirt and have someone in your family make an unknown shoeprint impression. See if you can find its source. How will you start the process? Try identifying the shoe with and without a cast. Which way reveals more details to you?

- shoebox
- dirt and water
- old shoe with a pattern on the sole
- hairspray
- powdered plaster of Paris
- paper cup

STEP

WELL, LOOKS LIKE A SWOOP AND I THINK I CAN MAKE OUT A NAME...

WHICH TOOL MADE THE MARK?

Many tools used at a crime scene leave behind a mark or impression. Tool marks can be scratches, cut marks, gouges, or even a "jimmy" mark or imprint of the tool left in a soft surface such as the wood in a door jam or a windowsill.

Enlist a friend or family member to help you make marks with different screwdrivers. Then, like a forensic scientist, you can observe and compare the marks to identify their source.

- **Find a way to label each screwdriver with a unique identifier, like a number or letter.** Ask a volunteer to choose one screwdriver (without telling you which one) and make an impression in a piece of clay. This is your crime scene tool impression.

- **Now you do the same with all four screwdrivers.** Be sure to keep track of which impression was made by the crime scene tool, and which screwdriver made each of the other impressions. If this information is not accurate, you won't be able to identify the correct tool.

- **Examining the four tool marks, do you observe identifying characteristics on each one?** Create a chart that lists the measurements and descriptions of each mark. Compare the four sample marks against the crime scene impression. Can you determine which screwdriver was used at the crime scene? Explain why you have come to your conclusion.

Ideas for Supplies ▼

- 4 flathead screwdrivers of similar size and style, but not identical
- masking tape
- marker
- a volunteer
- 5 pieces of clay
- magnifying glass
- ruler
- paper and pencil

To investigate more, add a mix of tools. Can you guess which tool made which mark? Try making prints using substances other than clay like fake blood, paint, or ketchup. Can you look at the different prints and determine which tools and even which screwdriver made them?

PRESS EACH OF THE TOOLS INTO THE CLAY FIRMLY.

FOOTPRINT CLUES

Investigators use footprints at a crime scene to reconstruct details of the events at the scene. They also use the prints to build a profile of the suspect. A person walking will leave different footprints than someone running or carrying a heavy object.

You can create a set of footprints to investigate how different factors affect a suspect's footprint and how it can reveal information to investigators.

Ideas for Supplies ▼

- a soft surface such as sand or mud that will hold a footprint
- several volunteers
- paper and pencil
- measuring tape and/or ruler

- **Ask each of your volunteers to walk across the soft surface.** Examining their footprints, notice how they differ. Make a chart to record your observations. How long is each person's stride? Do the stride lengths relate to the volunteers' leg lengths and weights? How else can you use the prints and stride to record characteristics about your suspect?

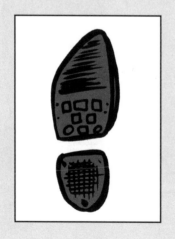

To investigate more, try the experiment with new variables. You could have your volunteers run, carry a heavy backpack, limp, skip, or hop. How do these changes affect the prints and stride? Now try it again without watching your volunteers in action. Can you examine the prints and guess how the suspect was moving and whether or not he or she carried extra weight?

Chapter 6 ▶
The Tiniest Clues: Trace Evidence

How do investigators find and use the smallest pieces of evidence?

>> No matter how careful criminals are, they usually leave behind something that an expert can pick up at a crime scene. It may be a single strand of hair, a tiny fragment of shattered glass, a clothing fiber, or a smudge of dirt.

Most criminals try not to leave evidence at the crime scene. They may wear gloves to avoid leaving fingerprints. They may wipe the floor to erase footprints or dispose of a weapon far from the scene. Forensic scientists are trained to discover and collect tiny clues called trace evidence. Using trace evidence, investigators can follow a trail straight to the suspect.

WHAT IS TRACE EVIDENCE?

Trace evidence is very small physical material. Hair, fibers, glass fragments, paint chips, dirt, and plant materials are all examples of trace evidence that investigators may find at a crime scene. These tiny, sometimes microscopic, pieces of evidence are transferred from person to person or between a person and a crime scene. They cling to clothes, shoes, or hair and can linger for months or years. This is an example of Locard's principle at work.

Even though trace evidence is small, it links a suspect to a place or to an object. But because it is usually so small, investigators must meticulously document, photograph, collect, and analyze trace evidence so that it does not become contaminated or unusable.

Trace evidence is generally considered class evidence. It can exclude a suspect, but usually does not individually connect a suspect to the crime. For example, if investigators find a blond hair at the crime scene, they can say with reasonable certainty that it did not come from a black-haired suspect. The blond hair does not point to one individual, but instead it narrows down the pool of suspects to people with blond hair.

At the crime lab, forensic scientists called trace evidence examiners analyze trace evidence by studying its physical and chemical properties. Physical properties describe the substance. How does it look, feel, and smell? Because most trace evidence cannot be seen clearly with the naked eye, trace evidence examiners use microscopes and other magnifying tools to observe the material. Chemical properties describe how a substance reacts when it is exposed to another material. What happens when it is mixed with water or another liquid? Since forensic scientists understand how known substances will react when combined with other materials, they can test the reaction of unknown substances to other materials and use their observations to identify the unknown substance.

CHEMICALS

Crime scene investigators often discover an unknown powder, liquid, or other substance at a crime scene. Identifying the substance helps investigators build a picture of the crime.

>> An unknown chemical could turn out to be a poison, drug, or other substance that is a critical piece of evidence.

FORENSIC CAREERS: FORENSIC TOXICOLOGIST

Forensic toxicology studies the effect of drugs and poisons on the human body in connection with medical and legal cases. As a member of the forensic team, the forensic toxicologist performs tests on samples collected by crime scene investigators. Their job is to identify any drugs or chemicals that may have been relevant to the crime and determine how the drugs or chemicals affected the suspect or victims. Forensic toxicologists are often called on to form opinions based on science and their own personal experience, and to testify in court.

The investigator starts by carefully observing the physical color, smell, and feel of the substance. The scientist tests its acidity, known as pH, and will determine other chemical properties of the substance by observing how it reacts when combined with known materials. Scientists know, for example, that if they combine a solution of formaldehyde and sulfuric acid with many opium substances such as morphine or heroin, it will turn purple.

FIBERS

Fibers are among the most commonly found pieces of trace evidence at crime scenes. Fibers are everywhere. They're found on any object made with fabric, including clothing, carpet, sheets, towels, upholstered furniture, or any object made with fabric. A fiber is the smallest unit of a textile material. It is spun with other fibers to create a yarn or thread that can be woven or knitted into a fabric. Fibers are easily shed and transported when they stick to clothing, skin, or hair.

Fibers can be natural or manmade. Natural fibers are made from animal, plant, or mineral material and can usually be identified easily under the microscope. The most common natural fiber is cotton, which has a distinctive twisted ribbon pattern. Other natural fibers include wool, mohair, cashmere, silk, hemp, and flax. Synthetic fibers are created to have certain properties that natural fibers do not offer, such as smoother texture or greater durability. Some of the most common synthetic fibers include rayon, nylon, and polyesters. By identifying a synthetic fiber found at a crime scene, a forensic scientist may be able to track down the manufacturer and match the fiber to a known source.

At the crime lab, trace evidence examiners use several tools and tests to identify an unknown fiber. Usually, scientists examine the fiber under a microscope, making note of its diameter, shape, color, shininess, curliness, and if there is any attached debris. Comparison microscopes are frequently used to examine two fibers side by side. Burning fibers may produce different types of ash, usually fine and soft or hard and beaded. The burning fiber may emit various smells and colors of smoke. Forensic scientists use all of these characteristics to identify an unknown fiber.

HAIR

Although a criminal may have been careful not to leave any fingerprints, it's much harder to prevent shedding a few hairs at the crime scene. Forensic scientists carefully collect hair and analyze it for its structure and chemical characteristics. Through chemical analysis, forensic scientists can identify toxins in the hair. If the hair follicle containing the root is still attached, they can also test for DNA.

Hair varies from person to person. Some people have fine, blond hair while others may have coarse, dark hair. On the same person, hair also varies from one body part to another. A hair from a person's head is different from hair found on the eyebrow or leg.

Each hair shaft has three parts. The cuticle is the outer coating of the hair, and has overlapping scales. The scales vary in thickness and pattern. Forensic scientists use the cuticles' scale pattern to determine if the hair is human or animal. The cuticle can also be used to match one hair to another. The hair's cortex holds the pigment that gives hair its color, and varies in thickness, texture, and color.

>> Fibers react to fire in different ways. Some may flare up and burn, while others curl, shrink, and melt. Burning fibers can help scientists identify them.

FORENSIC FACT

At a crime scene, the CSI combs the area for fibers. Both the victim's and the suspect's home and car are searched. Using tweezers, tape, or a vacuum, the CSI carefully collects fibers to send to the crime lab for analysis. Clothing from the victim, as well as from any suspect, is sent to the lab for trace evidence removal.

>> **Knowing where the hair came from is important, because in order to match one hair to another, an examiner must compare hairs from the same body part.**

AT THE LAB, THE HAIRS FOUND AT THE CRIME SCENE ARE ANALYZED AND DOCUMENTED.

LIVING ROOM SAMPLES SHOW 4 HAIR TYPES...

WAIT, 5!

Using a microscope, scientists can compare cortexes to match one hair to another. The medulla is the core of the hair and varies in thickness, whether it is continuous or broken, and opacity or how much light passes through it. Forensic scientists examine a hair's medulla to help identify different species.

Once a scientist has identified that a hair found at a crime scene is human, what's the next obvious question? Where did the hair come from on the body? Hairs from different areas of the body have different shapes. For example, head, eyebrow, and eyelash hairs have a more rounded cross-sectional shape. Armpit hair is more oval, while beard hair is triangular.

To identify a hair, investigators try to match it to a hair sample from a known source. Investigators take hair samples from the victim, suspects, family members, and any other people who may have been at the crime scene. Using a comparison microscope, they examine two hairs side-by-side, looking at the color, width, medulla pattern, pigment pattern, and cuticle pattern. A microscopic exam may also reveal tissue at the root of the hair. This suggests that the hair was ripped out forcibly instead of falling out naturally.

Although most hairs are class evidence, forensic analysis can sometimes tie a hair to an individual suspect. Tissue at the hair's root can hold DNA, which identifies an individual person. In addition, chemicals in a person's body often appear in the hair. Because two people rarely have the same amounts of chemicals in their body and hair, hair samples consisting of the same amount and types of chemicals are most likely from the same person.

GLASS

Glass is a common piece of evidence found at a crime scene. A suspect entering a crime scene can easily break a window, drop a vase, or shatter a glass bowl. When glass breaks at a crime scene, it scatters fragments around the area. Glass fragments easily transfer to a suspect's weapons, shoes, clothing, skin, and hair, creating a link to the crime scene. Working from the tiniest samples, glass experts can determine the type of glass and if it matches samples from a known source.

Many pieces of glass look identical to the naked eye. All glass is made by heating a mixture of sand, limestone, and soda ash, which is molded into shapes before it cools and hardens. But experts looking at two clear pieces of glass can find many properties that distinguish one piece from another.

To identify glass, scientists first visually examine the glass. They note the edge thickness, color, and if there are any labels or imprints on the glass. Glass differs depending on its purpose. Glass in a car window is different from glass in a cup. The thickness of the glass often indicates how it was used. Light bulb glass is thinner than window glass. Glass used in a door is even thicker because it is made to withstand the forces of the door opening and closing.

One of the most common ways to match glass samples is to determine the density of the glass. Density equals mass divided by volume. The density of two pieces of glass from the same source will always be the same, regardless of the size of the pieces.

FRACTURED GLASS

Sometimes, glass cracks but does not shatter. Forensic scientists can examine the pattern of cracks in the glass for clues to how it was broken. When a bullet or another object passes through glass, it may leave a hole with or without fracture lines. A bullet fractures glass in two ways. It leaves radial cracks, which spread out from the point of impact in a spoke-like pattern, or concentric cracks, which spread in a series of circles around the point of impact. Examining the hole can tell investigators the direction the bullet came from. On the impact side, the glass hole is clean, while on the other side, a small cone-shaped piece of glass may have been knocked out. If multiple bullets were fired, the fracture pattern can tell investigators the order of the bullets. Radial fractures do not cross fractures made by an earlier bullet.

>> The presence of the same types and amounts of added chemicals in two samples is evidence that the pieces of glass could have come from the same source.

FORENSIC FACT

The FBI has a database of refractive index values for approximately 2,000 types of glass. Forensic scientists can use this database to identify glass samples.

To measure density, forensic scientists put the glass sample into different liquids with known densities. If the glass floats, it is less dense. If it sinks, it is denser. The scientist continues to test the glass in different liquids until it finds a combination where the glass does not sink or float, but instead sits in the middle of two liquids. The density of the glass can then be calculated from the density of the two liquids.

Forensic scientists also use a glass sample's index of refraction to identify it. The index of refraction is a measure of how much light slows and bends as it passes through the glass. When light passes through any substance, it slows. The denser the substance, the more it slows and bends. More dense glass has a higher index of refraction and bends light more. Less dense glass has a lower index of refraction, bending light less. If two glass samples do not have the same index of refraction, they cannot have come from the same source. If both the density and refractive index of two samples of glass are the same, forensic scientists then compare the chemical composition of each sample.

Often, chemicals are added during glass manufacturing to change the characteristics of the finished product. Lead, for example, will make glass sparkle, boron gives it the ability to withstand extreme hot and cold, and cobalt will give it a blue color. In the manufacturing process, impurities can also enter the glass, which helps examiners match samples.

While glass fragments are generally considered class evidence, in some situations they can become individual evidence. If scientists can match a glass fragment with a fractured edge to a source with a missing piece, like fitting in a puzzle piece, the fragment can be individually linked to the source.

PAINT

Paint chips and smears often transfer from one object to another when the two make contact. A car may leave paint chips as it scrapes against a bench. A freshly painted window frame may transfer paint smears to a suspect's clothing or shoes during an escape. Finding the source of a paint chip or stain can reveal a clue that leads to a suspect.

To analyze a paint sample, a scientist first visually examines its physical characteristics and compares it to a control sample. If they match, the scientist will analyze the paint's chemical properties to match two samples. If the paint sample is multilayered, the scientists will look to see if the layers are in the same sequence and thicknesses. Like glass, a paint chip can be the missing piece of a jigsaw puzzle when matched to an area of missing paint. If that happens, what can be class evidence becomes individual evidence.

FORENSIC FACT

Paint contains many organic and inorganic properties, so it's more identifiable than glass. If a driver hits another car and flees the scene, forensic scientists can use a paint chip left on the victim's car from the collision to identify the make, model, and year of a suspect's car.

Sometimes, a forensic entomologist is called to a crime scene. Entomology is a branch of zoology that focuses on the study of insects. A forensic entomologist may be asked to collect and preserve insects as evidence. He may identify insects at different stages in the life cycle, such as eggs, larva, and adult. He may also be asked to use insect evidence to estimate how long a victim has been dead. When a person dies, the body begins to decompose. As this happens, bacteria and insects feed on the body. A forensic entomologist can use the type of insect found and its life cycle stage to estimate the stage of decomposition, and resulting time of death for the victim.

SOIL AND PLANTS

Soil evidence can be found at a crime scene or on a victim or suspect's shoes, clothes, car tires, or tools. Soil is a mixture of minerals, plant and animal matter, and other materials. Most soil also contains small pieces of manmade materials such as glass, paint, or concrete. Soil and its contents vary from area to area and region to region. The soil at a local playground may be very different than the soil behind a suspect's house. Finding where soil came from can help investigators retrace a suspect or victim's movements and link a suspect to a crime scene. If investigators discover shoes in a suspect's car with soil stains that match the soil at the crime scene, they can link the suspect to the scene.

Investigators carefully collect soil samples to be analyzed at the crime lab. First, forensic scientists visually inspect the soil through a microscope. They observe the color and consistency. They look for substances such as plant material, animal hairs, or seeds that may link the soil to a particular location. If a soil sample includes a leaf from a plant that is native to a specific area, it narrows down where the sample could have originated. Investigators search for leaves, stems, pine needles, bark, flower petals, seeds, and pollen to help identify the source of a soil sample.

Chemical analysis can determine whether the pH and mineral content of two samples match. Imagine a suspect lives in a neighborhood with a specific soil makeup and that type of soil is found at the crime scene or on the victim. This type of soil evidence can link a suspect to a crime.

INDEX OF REFRACTION

The index of refraction of glass is another physical property that scientists use to identify glass at a crime scene and match it to its source. The index of refraction is a measure of how much light bends as it passes through glass. Denser glass has a higher index of refraction. Light bends more as it passes through the dense glass. This experiment will illustrate how different materials have a different index of refraction.

Ideas for Supplies ▼

- clear glass bowl
- smaller Pyrex glass bowl or cup
- water
- vegetable oil

- **With water in the glass bowl, place the smaller bowl inside it.** Even though all the items are clear, you should be able to see the bowl, water, and Pyrex bowl separately because each has a different index of refraction and bends light differently.

- **Empty the larger glass bowl. Pour about 2 cups of vegetable oil into it (475 milliliters) and place the Pyrex bowl in the oil.** What do you see? Record your observations. What explanation do you have for what you observed? Do you think the water or the oil has a higher index of refraction? Which is the denser liquid?

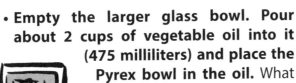

LIGHT SOURCE

WHICH ONE SHOULD I USE?

> **To investigate more, repeat the experiment using a small glass bowl that is not made from Pyrex. What is the result and why?**

SOIL ANALYSIS

Dirt is easily tracked to and from a crime scene. Forensic scientists analyze dirt evidence to reveal clues about a suspect's or victim's movement. Soil analysis can also match soil found at the scene to items in the suspect's possession or in his or her backyard. Scientists use many methods to compare, identify, and match soil samples. In this experiment, you will use a technique called soil layering to compare and contrast samples from different locations.

- **You're going to test soil samples from four different locations.** Collecting about 3 cups of dirt from each location should be enough (720 milliliters). Seal the samples in plastic bags, labeling where you found each one.

- **Spread a small amount of each type of soil on white paper for contrast, and use a magnifying glass to examine the dirt.** What do you notice? Create a table and record your observations.

- **Label each glass jar or plastic soda bottle with one soil location and fill them half full with the corresponding soil sample.** Add water until the containers are nearly full and seal them. Shake the jars vigorously for about 30 seconds and then let them sit for a full day.

- **Observe the layers in each jar.** What do you see? How many layers are there? How do the layers from each sample compare to the other samples?

To investigate more, scoop out some material from the different layers and spread it on a paper towel. Use a magnifying glass to examine the dirt closely. What additional information can you see about the layers? Does each soil type have something unique to identify it? Have a volunteer scoop a sample without telling you its source. Can you identify which jar the sample came from?

Ideas for Supplies ▼

- shovel
- measuring cups
- 4 ziplock plastic bags
- permanent marker
- black and white paper
- 4 large glass jars or plastic soda bottles with lids
- funnel
- water
- magnifying glass
- pencil and paper

FIBER BURN ANALYSIS

Everywhere you go, you leave fibers from your clothing and pick up fibers from furniture, carpet, car seats, and other fabric you contact. Forensic scientists carefully examine fibers found at a crime scene to help identify suspects or victims and trace where they have been. Because fibers react differently to fire, one way scientists identify fibers is to observe how they burn.

Caution: Wear safety goggles during this investigation. Adult supervision is required when using a flame.

- **Using natural and manmade fabric samples from home or a local fabric store, separate a single fiber or thread of each fabric and place it on a piece of paper.** White paper works best for darker colors and dark paper contrasts best with light-colored thread.

- **Make a wet mount slide to study the fibers closely with a magnifying glass or a microscope.** Place each fiber on a slide with a drop of water. This makes it easier to see. Create an evidence log and record or sketch your observations and descriptions of each fiber.

WOW! WE HAVE SO MANY FIBERS TO ANALYZE! SO EXCITING.

- **Before you burn anything, place a bowl of water next to where you will light the candle.** If any fibers burn out of control, you can quickly drop them into the bowl of water to extinguish the flame. You can also dip your tweezers into the water if they get too hot from the candle.

- **Using tweezers, hold one of the fibers near the flame, but not directly in the flame.** Observe what happens. Does the fiber melt, curl, or catch fire? Record your observations in your evidence log.

- **Without placing your hand or tweezers directly above the flame (because it will rise), what happens if you move the fiber into the flame?** How does it react? Does it light slowly or quickly? Does it melt, flicker, or pop? Record your observations.

- **Remove the fiber from the flame.** Does it extinguish immediately or does it continue to burn, smoke, or glow? Does it have an odor? What does it look like? What do its ashes look like? Examine the burnt fiber with the magnifying glass. Record your observations.

- **What differences did you observe among the different fiber types?** Was there a general difference between synthetic and natural fibers? How could you use these observations to identify an unknown fiber at a crime scene?

> To investigate more, prepare another set of slides but don't label them. Mix them up until you are sure you can't remember which slide came from which source. Are you able to use your evidence log to identify the fibers? Can you identify some just by looking at the slides? Do you need to observe their burning properties to tell them apart?

Ideas for Supplies ▼

- fibers or threads from several different-colored fabrics such as wool, cotton, rayon, silk, polyesters
- tweezers
- white and colored paper
- paper and pencil
- magnifying glass
- microscope (optional)
- glass slides and cover slips (optional)
- safety goggles
- candle
- matches
- bowl of water

MYSTERY POWDER: PHYSICAL AND CHEMICAL ANALYSIS

Forensic scientists will often be asked to identify trace physical evidence that is unidentified. A powdery substance could be a drug, a poison, or simply baby powder. Physical properties describe how a substance looks and feels. Chemical properties are used to describe how a substance reacts when it encounters another substance. In this experiment, you will observe the physical properties of several substances and look for their chemical properties when mixed with water and vinegar in order to identify a mystery powder. Before you get started, you'll want to create an evidence chart to record your observations for this experiment.

- paper and pencil
- flour
- cornstarch
- baking soda
- spoons
- black construction paper
- paper cups
- magnifying glass
- water
- vinegar
- marker

- **Place a small amount of the powder onto a sheet of black construction paper.** Use a magnifying glass to carefully examine the appearance and texture of the substance, and record your observations.

- **For each powder, record what you see when you combine 1 tablespoon of powder (5 milliliters) in a paper cup with 3 tablespoons of water (15 milliliters).** Does the mixture change color, texture, or leave a residue? Does the powder dissolve in water or sink to the bottom?

- **What if you combine the powder with white vinegar instead of water?** Observe and record what happens. What differences do you observe in the physical and chemical properties of each substance that would help forensic scientists identify an unknown powder found at a crime scene?

To investigate more, keep adding new substances to your test. Try salt, sugar, baking powder, or lemonade mix. Predict what will happen when you combine each one first with water and then with vinegar. What properties do you observe? How accurate were your predictions?

CHEMICAL ANALYSIS FLAME TEST

One way forensic scientists observe the chemical properties of an unknown substance is to test how it reacts to a flame. A flame test can identify some of the basic elements in a chemical, helping scientists identify the substance. When performing your own chemical flame test, be sure to conduct the experiment in a well-ventilated area with an adult present.

You will start by testing how alcohol reacts to a flame. Alcohol will be your known chemical. Then you'll add other chemicals to the alcohol and see what happens. To prepare, make an observation chart. Then fill a glass cup or bowl with water to keep nearby for extinguishing flames.

Caution: Wear safety goggles and be very careful using a flame with rubbing alcohol, which is very flammable. Adult supervision is required when using a flame.

- **Pour a small amount of rubbing alcohol into a paper cup (5 milliliters) and soak one end of a cotton swab in it.** Because rubbing alcohol is very flammable, make sure you replace the lid on the bottle immediately. Before you light the candle, move the alcohol bottle at least 6 feet away (2 meters).

- **Holding the dry end of the cotton swab, quickly pass the other end through the flame so the tip catches on fire.** Carefully observe its colors. Is the color the same throughout? Drop the swab into the bowl of water. Then record your observations.

- **Now test the other additives, starting with a tablespoon of table salt (5 milliliters).** Always use a fresh paper cup and a fresh cotton swab. After you observe the flame, drop the swab into the bowl of water and record your observations. The metals in the substances you test cause the flame to produce colors. What colors did each of these metals produce? How does a flame test help forensic scientists identify each substance?

To investigate more, compare the flames from each substance that you tested. Did any of the flames appear to have similar colors? What explains this result?

Ideas for Supplies ▼

- safety goggles
- water
- measuring spoons
- 90 percent Isopropyl or rubbing alcohol
- paper cups
- cotton swabs
- candle
- matches
- table salt (sodium chloride)
- salt substitute (potassium chloride)
- de-icer (calcium chloride)
- cream of tartar (potassium chloride)
- plaster of Paris (calcium sulfate)
- powdered roach killer (boric acid)

FIND THE DENSITY OF GLASS

Different types of glass have different physical characteristics, allowing scientists to distinguish glass from different sources. Forensic scientists analyze the glass to determine what type of glass it is and where it came from. They measure the physical properties of the glass to help identify and match it. One common test measures the density of glass. Density is an identifying characteristic of glass, because two pieces of glass from the same source will have the same density.

GLASS MARBLES

SCALE

WATER

VARIOUS PIECES OF GLASS

- **Remember that density is mass divided by volume.** You're going to start by finding the mass of your samples. Simply weigh each piece on the scale and record the weight or mass.

- **Now you need the volume. You can find this by seeing how much water your samples displace.** For each piece, start with 20 milliliters of water in the graduated cylinder and then add the glass sample. If 20 milliliters does not cover your sample, remove the glass and add more water, making sure to record the new measurement. Read the new volume measure on the side of the cylinder (X). Calculate the volume of the fragment as follows: Volume = X − 20 milliliters (use the actual amount of water you used if it was more than 20 milliliters). Record the volume.

- **Calculate the density of your samples.** If water has a density of 1 gram per milliliter, do the samples have a higher or lower density? Create a bar graph showing the density of each sample. Which samples had similar densities? Which were most different?

> To investigate more, try different sizes of the same type of glass. Do you have a large drinking glass and a small juice cup made of the same glass? Or two different sizes of the same marbles? Does the density change with different-sized samples?

Ideas for Supplies

- paper and pencil
- scale or balance
- glass samples such as a marble, eyedropper (without rubber end), test tube, small cup
- graduated cylinder
- water
- calculator

STUDY HAIRS

Forensic scientists carefully examine hair found at a crime scene. They study the hair's diameter and how smooth or coarse it is. They examine it for patterns and characteristics that identify the hair as human or animal. Hairs can exclude suspects if they do not match and can narrow the pool of possible suspects. Using a microscope, see how forensic scientists examine hair and use it to link a suspect to a crime scene.

Can you convince some brave volunteers to pull out two hair samples each from their heads for you? Your project is worth a quick moment of pain!

- **Create a microscope slide for each hair.** You can use either a dry or a wet mount. For a dry mount, simply place the hair on the slide and put the cover slip on top. To create a wet mount slide, place the hair on the slide, and add a drop of water before you put the cover slip in place. The water should not bubble out the sides. Make two full sets of slides, each including one hair from each volunteer. Whenever you're working with different samples, it's extremely important to label everything carefully.

- **Examine each hair from the first set of slides.** Look for specific characteristics that might help you identify the hair. Is it curly or straight? Can you see the shape of the cross-section? Making a sketch can help. What differences do you note among the samples? How can these differences be used to identify a suspect or match a hair found at a crime scene?

- **Select a slide from the second sample set.** Without looking to see which volunteer it came from, can you match it to the correct volunteer?

Ideas for Supplies ▼

- microscope slides and cover slips for each volunteer
- eyedropper and water (optional)
- small stickers to label microscope slides
- hairs from the heads of several volunteers
- microscope
- paper
- colored pencils

To investigate more, examine pet hair. What differences do you observe between pet hair and human hair? How could forensic scientists use this information to exclude pet hairs found at the crime scene? What about comparing hair samples from different parts of your own body? How does hair from your arm (ouch!) differ from hair from your head?

WOW, MARCO'S HAIR IS MUCH ROUGHER THAN SARAH'S...

Chapter 7 ▶
Fakes and Forgeries

How do experts use written or electronic documents to help solve a crime?

>> Handwriting analysis as a forensic science is based on the fact that every person in the world has a unique way of writing.

FORENSIC FACT

A document may be broadly defined as anything that bears marks, signs, or symbols that have meaning or convey a message to someone.

Threatening letters, ransom notes, counterfeit checks, and other documents can be clues to a crime. These types of documents become evidence in a forensic investigation. Yet documents are not always what they appear to be. To rely on a document as evidence, an investigator must authenticate it. To do this, a forensic document examiner closely analyzes a document to find out who wrote or printed it, when it was created, and if it is genuine.

HANDWRITING: UNIQUE AND PERSONAL

We all learn to write from a young age and develop our own unique, personal style. No two people write the exact same way. Handwriting styles may look similar at first glance, but under closer examination, unique variations mark each person's script as his or her own.

You may remember being taught your ABCs in school using a particular style of writing. Many children begin writing in a similar style to that of other kids of the same age in the same school or area. As children mature, their writing styles develop and evolve. By the time kids reach their late teens, their writing styles have become an unconscious and automatic action. They have developed the individual characteristics that are unique to their own writing and that distinguish their writing from anyone else's. While two people may have some of the same individual characteristics, it is extremely unlikely that the same two people would share 20 or more individual characteristics in their writing.

You've likely noticed that even your own handwriting can vary. And as you age, you'll start to notice your handwriting changing. We do not write the same way every time we put pen to paper. Different conditions, pens, paper, and positions affect handwriting. A person writing with a pen and paper while seated at a desk will write differently than when standing up to write on a chalkboard with chalk. Handwriting may be temporarily or permanently affected by health conditions such as Parkinson's disease, stroke, fatigue, stress, impaired vision, and injury to the hand or arm.

FORENSIC CAREERS: FORENSIC DOCUMENT EXAMINER

A forensic document examiner is a specialist called in when a document's source or authenticity is in question. The forensic document examiner analyzes the document, its paper, source marks, ink, and any handwriting. He or she looks for signs of alteration and forgery. If sample documents are available, he or she compares handwriting or typing to determine who produced it. Using microscopic, photographic, and chemical analysis, the document examiner also attempts to identify the document's paper and ink and to reveal any damaged or obliterated writing.

HANDWRITING ANALYSIS

Handwriting analysis is a long, methodical process. Examiners study how people form each letter and determine which characteristics are unique. Analysts distinguish between style and individual characteristics. Two people might share a similar writing style, but it is the individual characteristics that analysts study to identify who wrote a document.

To identify handwriting, analysts compare a document in question against a writing sample, called an exemplar, from a known source. A ransom note may be compared to a writing sample from a suspect. A grandfather's will may be compared against a letter he wrote to his wife. Writing samples can be nonrequested or requested. Nonrequested samples already exist and are known to be authentic. They are considered the best for comparison since they aren't prepared for purposes of examination. They reveal a lot about the writer's true style as well as words and phrases the writer commonly uses.

If nonrequested samples do not exist or cannot be authenticated, the examiner will ask the suspected writer to create a requested writing sample. A requested sample has the benefit of being authentic since there is no doubt who wrote it.

The examiner will have the writer use a writing instrument and paper that is similar to what was used in the questioned document. The writer will be asked for cursive or block printing based on what is used in the questioned document. The examiner can also instruct the writer to use specific words or phrases that are in the questioned document to compare them to the sample.

If a writer is nervous while preparing a requested sample, it can affect his or her handwriting. Sometimes a writer will intentionally try to disguise the writing. By requesting a large sample, examiners can make it more difficult for a writer to do this. It can be nearly impossible to alter individual handwriting characteristics consistently throughout a large document.

ANALYZING A SAMPLE

Using a microscope to study each word and letter closely, the examiner studies the handwriting in both documents, looking for a wide variety of individual characteristics that fall into several categories:

- **Letter form analyzes** the overall size, shape, curve, and slant of letters, as well as the proportion of letters in relation to each other. The examiner will look at how the writer uses beginning and ending strokes for each letter and how the writer connects letters.

- **Line form analyzes** how smooth and dark the overall lines of writing appear, and the amount of pressure the writer uses.

- **Formatting analyzes** the margins the writer uses on the paper, the spacing between letters and words, the spacing between lines, and the placement of words on a line.

- **Content analyzes** how the writer uses grammar, punctuation, and words. Does the writer repeat certain words or phrases? Are there consistent errors or misspellings?

A handwriting examiner will compare the two samples, looking for similarities and differences. No one single feature will cause two samples to match. Instead, it takes a combination of similar characteristics before an examiner will conclude that the same person authored the two documents.

Cursive writing is easier to identify than printed writing because it has more distinguishing features.

FORENSIC FACT

What happens if a suspect refuses to give a sample of their writing? A judge can order a suspect to produce a handwriting sample if he or she refuses.

>> Handwriting analysis is so subjective it is not always accepted in court as evidence. But computer analysis that digitally compares scanned documents is increasingly accurate.

FORGERY

Sometimes a forensic document examiner is asked to determine if a document is a forgery. Forgery is a serious crime involving writing or altering a document intending to defraud or deceive. Faked signatures often show up on blank checks. Forgers usually try to fake a person's signature as best as possible free hand. Other times, they place another document over the original and trace its lines.

Document alterations can be as simple as changing a single number or date, or they can be extremely complicated, like changing signatures or large sections of text. A forger may try to alter a will to inherit significantly more money. A thief may try to alter an attendance sheet to establish an alibi at the time of a theft.

Several clues can tip off an examiner that a document is a forgery. Sometimes forgers leave evidence of previous marks, such as tracing lines. Forger's tremors are fine, shaky marks that can occur when a forger tries to copy someone's signature or handwriting. Uneven writing speed and pressure, hesitations, unusual pen lifts, and blunt beginnings and endings are all signs a forger has been at work.

When examining a document for authenticity, the examiner will look for traces of erasure, or words that have been removed. They can examine the document with a magnifying glass or under an ultraviolet light to expose erasure marks or fragments of a rubber eraser. Some powders also cling to rubber particles, revealing places where something has been erased. If an examiner discovers a site where something was erased, he or she is able to prove that the document has been altered.

>> Forgeries range from faking a signature to altering entire sections of documents.

ELECTRONIC DOCUMENTS

Since so many documents today are printed or copied, forensic document examiners also study documents for individual characteristics that might identify where the document was generated. Printers, typewriters, and copy machines can leave marks when feeding a paper through the machine. Inks and toners can also be analyzed to identify the document's source. Printers can have imbedded characteristics that tell investigators which printer created a document. Examiners can use this information to determine if a document is genuine or a fake.

A criminal might use chemicals to remove writing. Using a microscope, the examiner can see remnants of ink or a discoloration where paper was treated with chemicals. If a laser was used to erase words, the paper's fibers will show damage when examined under a microscope.

A forgery might involve adding writing to a document. For example, someone might change the amount of a check by adding a few zeroes or change a date from 2/15/2012 to 12/15/2012. Under a microscope, the examiner will look for subtle differences between the original writing or print and the added writing, such as changes in ink color, line thickness, or pen pressure. An ultraviolet or infrared light can show ink differences, causing some to fluoresce while others fade.

PAPER AND INK ANALYSIS

Some types of paper have a watermark, which offers examiners a simple way to identify a paper's brand and type. But it isn't usually that easy. Forensic document examiners frequently need to analyze the paper content and the ink used in a document. Paper variations can reveal if entire pages were added to a document or prove a document could not have been created when it was supposed to have been.

All paper is made of wood and cotton. But chemicals are added in manufacturing that affect color, brightness, strength, and other properties. By testing the chemical makeup of paper, an examiner can sometimes narrow down its type and manufacturer. Different manufacturers also use specific combinations of chemicals in their inks. Forensic examiners test ink using a process called chromatography, which separates the components of inks and dyes. This allows experts to match an ink to its source.

FORENSIC FACT

The United States Secret Service and the Internal Revenue Service National Forensic Laboratory jointly maintain the largest known forensic collection of writing inks in the world, which is comprised of over 8,500 ink standards dating back to the 1920s.

INK CHROMATOGRAPHY

Forensic scientists use chromatography or the physical separation of a mixture into individual components to identify and match the inks and dyes used in markers and pens. Although several black pens may appear to make the same markings, a chromatography test may show distinct variations that can be used to find the author and source of written evidence.

You're going to investigate how dye colors separate and why chromatography works using water-soluble black markers. You'll be amazed at how many dyes are found in just one small black line.

- It will be important in this experiment to keep track of which pen you are using on which coffee filter, so remember to label everything. Label each pen with a number and, working with four strips of filter paper, label the top of each strip with a pen number. Draw a thick line on each one about ¼ inch up from the bottom (½ centimeter) using the appropriate pen.

- Place a small amount of water in four large cups. Tape the top of each filter strip to a pencil and hang the strips so the bottom of the paper touches the water, but not the marker line.

- Take the paper out after 5 minutes and let it dry. What happened to the black lines? Create a chart to record your observations. What colors did you observe for each marker? What differences and similarities did you see? Did the colors separate in the same order? How could scientists use this information to match written evidence to a pen in the suspect's possession?

- coffee filters
- scissors
- 4 black markers (not permanent markers)
- masking tape
- pencils
- 4 large cups
- water
- paper and pencil

To investigate more, you can experiment using anything with dye. Many candies, like M&Ms, Skittles, or Reese's Pieces, contain artificial dye. You'll need to let the candy's color dissolve in water first by placing a piece of candy on a paper plate with a drop of water. Then you can dab the colored water onto a vertical filter strip and stand it in a glass with ½ inch of water. Check the paper at time intervals. What does it look like at 15 minutes? 30 minutes? An hour? Now you know why you should eat red strawberries, orange oranges, and blue blueberries. Their colors are all natural!

FIND THE FORGERY

Signing another person's name is a common type of forgery. Handwriting analysts are often asked to examine a signature on a contract, will, or other document to verify that it is authentic.

In this investigation, you will use principles of handwriting analysis to determine if a signature is real or a fake. Make sure your volunteers know not to try this in real life or they could find themselves in a lot of trouble!

• **Ask one volunteer to create an authentic signature document by signing his or her name on a blank piece of paper.** Then, ask the same volunteer to sign a second, identical piece of paper. Label the back of the first signature "authentic" and the back of the second signature "real."

- **See how well your second volunteer can forge the authentic signature. What will that volunteer need to prepare?** The same pen and paper? A familiarity with the signature he or she will attempt? Ask the volunteer to try a freehand forgery of the authentic signature and then to make a second attempt by tracing the authentic signature. Label the back of both forgeries as "fake."

- **Shuffle the one real and two fake samples so you don't know which is real and which are forged.** Examine all three and compare them against the authentic signature. Does a magnifying glass help? Which one do you think is real and which two are forgeries? What handwriting characteristics led you to your conclusion? Which is closer, the freehand attempt or the tracing?

To investigate more, try having a volunteer change something in an existing document. See if you can examine the document closely and discover what has been changed.

HANDWRITING ANALYSIS

Some people have handwriting with fancy swirls. Others write all in caps or mix printing and cursive. Handwriting experts can use these unique characteristics to examine a handwriting sample and compare it to a questioned sample.

- **Recruit some friends to make samples for you. Give each volunteer a number.** Ask them each to write the same thing on two separate cards and label the back with their number. For example, they could each write, "Your handwriting is as unique as your fingerprints." The same pen should be used for all of the writing samples.

- **Carefully examine one writing sample from each volunteer.** Analyze and describe the unique characteristics of each. Record your observations.

  a. Are the lines smooth or shaky?

  b. Are the words written close together or farther apart?

  c. Does the size of the letters vary or stay the same?

  d. How are the letters connected? Are there pen lifts and separations?

  e. How are capital letters connected to lowercase letters?

  f. How do words or letters begin and end?

  g. Are there any unusual letter formations, such as tails, cursive and print combinations, or flourishes?

  h. Is the writing light or dark?

  i. Does the writing slant?

  j. Is the writing above or below the line?

- **Mix up the second set of samples and try to match them with the first.**

- several volunteers
- pen and index cards
- paper and pencil

To investigate more, challenge yourself. Ask your volunteers to bring you a nonrequested sample of anything they have written. Without knowing who wrote the samples, see if you can identify each sample's author.

WHOA, JAN'S HANDWRITING IS UM...YEAH... INTERESTING.

▾ GLOSSARY

algor mortis: the cooling of the body after death.

alibi: a form of defense against an accusation in which the accused person claims or proves that he or she was somewhere else at the time that a crime was committed.

amino acid: an organic compound that is used in every cell of the body to build proteins needed for survival.

anatomy: the study of the physical structure of living things.

anthropology: the study of human culture and human development.

arch: a ridge pattern that looks like a hill.

artery: a blood vessel that carries blood from the heart to the rest of the body.

assailant: a person who attacks another.

authenticate: to establish as genuine.

autolysis: the digestion of cells by their own enzymes.

autopsy: the inspection and dissection of a dead body.

bacteria: tiny organisms found in animals, plants, soil, and water.

ballistics: the study of the motion of bullets and indentification of their distinctive characteristics after being fired to match bullets or fragments to specific weapons.

biological evidence: organic evidence such as hair, saliva, and blood.

biology: the study of life and of living things.

blood spatter: a collection of blood spots that may be different sizes and shapes.

cartilage: elastic, flexible tissue in the body.

cause of death: the specific reason a person died.

cell: the basic unit of a living thing.

chain of custody: the order in which evidence from a crime scene is handled by investigators.

chemical properties: how a substance reacts when it is exposed to another material.

chemistry: the study of the properties of substances and how they react with one another.

chromatography: a technique of separating the components of a liquid such as ink.

class evidence: evidence that narrows the pool of suspects but does not point to one individual.

clot: to form a semi-solid mass of blood.

concentric cracks: cracks that form a series of circles in glass around the point of impact.

contact bloodstain: a bloodstain caused when a wet, bloody object comes in contact with another surface.

contaminate: to make impure or dirty by contact or mixture with another substance.

continuous: uninterrupted.

contradict: to state the opposite of someone else's statement.

control samples: samples from known people or objects, taken to compare against evidence recovered at the crime scene.

coroner: a public official formerly responsible for investigating deaths that appear not to have natural causes. Coroners have been replaced by medical examiners.

corpse: a dead body.

correlation: a connection or relationship between two or more things.

cortex: the part of the hair that holds pigment.

crime: an action that is against the law, or a failure to act that is required by law.

crime scene: the location of a crime.

criminal: a person who commits a crime.

CSI: stands for crime scene investigation or crime scene investigators. The CSI's job is to document the crime scene and collect physical evidence.

cuticle: the outer coating of the hair shaft.

deceive: to intentionally trick or mislead someone.

decomposition: the rotting of organic matter.

defendant: a person accused of a crime.

defraud: to cheat someone out of something.

delta: a point in a fingerprint ridge pattern that looks like the Greek letter delta.

density: the mass of an object divided by its volume.

diameter: the distance across a circle through the middle.

displace: to move something from its place or to replace fluid with an object.

district attorney: an elected or appointed official who represents the government when prosecuting a crime.

DNA: deoxyribonucleic acid. The substance found in your cells that carries your genetic information, the "blueprint" of who you are.

enzyme: a natural chemical that causes a reaction.

evidence: the available facts or information supporting or denying a theory.

evolve: to change or develop slowly, over time.

exemplar: a writing sample.

eyewitness: a person who sees an act or event and can give a firsthand account of it.

false positive: a test result that incorrectly returns a positive result.

femur: the upper leg bone.

fibers: thin threads.

fibula: the outer bone below the knee.

fingerprint: the unique pattern of ridges on a fingertip.

fluorescent: a bright color that seems to reflect light.

forensic anthropologist: a scientist who studies bones and human remains at a crime scene.

forensic entomologist: a scientist who studies insects and their role at a crime scene, particularly in a death investigation.

forensic odontologist: a scientist who uses teeth, bite marks, and dental records to identify a victim or suspect.

forensic pathologist: a doctor who examines bodies to determine the cause and manner of death.

forensic serologist: a scientist who performs chemical and biological tests on blood samples found at a crime scene.

forensic toxicologist: a scientist who tests for the presence of drugs and chemicals as part of a crime scene investigation.

forensics: the science of finding and analyzing crime scene evidence.

forgery: writing or altering a document with the intent to defraud.

fragment: a tiny broken piece of something.

friction ridge: a raised line on a person's finger pad that gives fingers traction and create a fingerprint pattern.

gelatinous: having the consistency of jelly.

genuine: real.

gravity: the force that pulls all objects to the earth's surface.

hemoglobin: the oxygen-carrying protein in red blood cells.

human remains: a dead person's body.

humerus: the arm bone between the shoulder and elbow.

hypothesis: an unproven idea that tries to explain certain facts or observations.

impressed print: a visible, three-dimensional print made when a person touches a soft substance such as mud or wax.

GLOSSARY

impressions: marks or indentations made by pressure.

index of refraction: a measure of how much light slows and bends as it passes through an object such as glass or water.

infer: to conclude from evidence and reasoning.

inference: arriving at a conclusion.

inorganic: not part of the living world, such as metal and glass.

larva: the wormlike stage in an insect's life.

laser: a device that emits a focused beam of light.

latent print: an invisible print made from oils, perspiration, and other skin substances.

loop: a ridge pattern that begins and ends on the same side of the print.

manner of death: the cause that triggered the sequence of events that led to a person's death.

medical examiner: a medical official who investigates deaths and injuries in crimes.

medulla: the core of a hair.

microscopic: something so small that it can only be seen with a microscope.

minutiae point: a specific point in a fingerprint ridge pattern where ridges end or two ridges meet.

molecule: the simplest part of an element (like oxygen) or a compound (like water). Molecules are made up of combinations of atoms, which are the smallest particles of matter.

negative footprint: a three-dimensional depression left when a person steps on a soft surface.

nonrequested sample: a writing sample already exists and is known to be authentic.

nucleus: the central part of a cell.

nutrients: the substances in food and soil that keep animals and plants healthy and growing.

organic: something that is or was living, such as animals, wood, paper, grass, and insects.

osteons: tiny tubes in bone that hold blood vessels.

passive bloodstain: a blood stain made by the force of gravity.

patent print: a visible, two-dimensional print made when a person touches a substance such as ink or blood.

pathology: the study of disease.

perimeter: the outer border of an area.

pH: a measure of acidity or alkalinity, on a scale from 0 to 14.

physical evidence: objects at the scene of the crime, on the victim, or in a suspect's possession.

physical properties: characteristics of a substance without it being exposed to any other material.

physics: the study of physical forces, including matter, energy, and motion, and how these forces interact with each other.

pigment: the coloring of something.

plasma: the liquid part of blood.

platelets: a small body found in plasma that promotes blood clotting.

point of similarity: a point where a minutiae point on two different prints matches.

porous: full of many little holes.

positive print: a two-dimensional mark left by a dirty shoe on a hard surface.

preliminary: an early or introductory action that is not final.

presumptive: giving a reasonable basis to believe something is true.

primary crime scene: the original location of a crime or accident.

profile: a sketch or list of a suspect's characteristics.

projected bloodstain: a bloodstain caused when a force other than gravity is applied to blood.

property: a characteristic quality or distinctive feature of something.

prosecutor: a lawyer who represents the state or the people in a criminal trial.

protein: a compound found in many foods such as meat and eggs that we and other animals need to survive.

puberty: when a child's body develops into an adult body.

putrefaction: to decay, with a foul smell.

questioned document: a document that needs to be verified as genuine and not altered.

radial cracks: cracks that spread out in glass from the point of impact in a spoke-like pattern.

radius: the lower arm bone on the thumb side.

requested writing sample: a writing sample that investigators obtain from a suspect.

rigor mortis: body stiffness after death.

sciatic notch: a notch in the hip bone.

search warrant: a court order that allows police to search a property.

secondary crime scene: an alternate location where additional evidence may be found.

serum: a clear yellow liquid that separates when blood clots.

species: a group of plants or animals that are closely related and look the same.

sphere: a three-dimensional round shape, like a ball.

striation: a pattern of parallel grooves or narrow bands.

subjective: based on somebody's opinions or feelings rather than on facts or evidence.

suspect: a person who might be guilty.

technology: tools, methods, and systems used to solve a problem or do work.

testimonial evidence: oral or written statements and court testimony by people who witnessed an event.

testimony: the statement of a witness, usually under oath in court.

tibia: the thicker inner leg bone below the knee.

tissue: a large number of cells similar in form and function that are grouped together, such as muscle tissue.

trace evidence: small but measurable items such as fibers, skin cells, powders, or soil.

trajectory: the curve or line taken by an object moving through space.

tread: the outer part of a tire that makes contact with the ground.

vein: a blood vessel that carries blood to the heart.

velocity: the rate of speed at which something travels.

vertebrate: an animal with a backbone.

victim: somebody hurt or killed.

whorl: a ridge pattern that forms a spiral that looks like a complete circle.

▾ RESOURCES

↳ MUSEUMS AND SCIENCE CENTERS

National Museum of Crime and Punishment, Washington, DC
Includes a crime lab, simulated shooting range, and numerous interactive exhibits.
http://www.crimemuseum.org/

Museum of Osteology, Oklahoma City, Oklahoma
Displays hundreds of skulls and skeletons from around the world. *http://www.museumofosteology.org/*

Smithsonian Museum of Natural History, Washington, DC
Features a Written in Bone exhibition through January 2014 that highlights the work of forensic anthropologists.
http://anthropology.si.edu/writteninbone/index.html

↳ BOOKS

DNA and Blood: Dead People Do Tell Tales
Sara Latta, Enslow, 2011.

Famous Forensic Cases
John Townsend, Franklin Watts, 2011.

Forensics Colin Hynson, Smart Apple Media, 2011.

The Forensic Casebook
N.E. Genge, Random House, 2002.

Forensics for Dummies D.P. Lyle, MD, Wiley, 2004.

Forensic Science
Christopher Cooper, DK Eyewitness Books, 2008.

Forensic Secrets
John Townsend, Franklin Watts, 2012.

On the Scene: A CSI's Life
Diana Herweck, Time for Kids, 2012.

Written in Bone: Buried Lives of Jamestown and Colonial Maryland Sally M. Walker, Carolrhoda Books, 2009.

↳ FORENSIC EXPERIMENTS

Crime Scene Science Fair Projects
Elizabeth Snoke Harris, Lark Books, 2006.

CSI Expert! Forensic Science for Kids
Karen K. Schultz, Prufrock Press, 2008.

Fingerprints: Crime-Solving Science Experiments
Kenneth G. Rainis, Enslow, 2006.

Forensic Science Experiments
Aviva Ebner, Chelsea House, 2011.

Science Fair Winners: Crime Scene Science
Karen Romano Young, National Geographic, 2009.

↳ WEB SITES

Crime Scene Investigation
Information about the job of a CSI and the science used in an investigation.
http://idahoptv.org/dialogue4kids/season12/csi/facts.cfm

DNA
DNA and how it can be used to identify a suspect.
http://scienceforkids.kidipede.com/biology/cells/dna.htm

Explore Forensics
Articles and explanations about a variety of forensic topics. *www.exploreforensics.co.uk/*

Fingerprint Ridge Patterns
Examples of fingerprint ridge patterns and minutiae points. *http://sciencespot.net/Media/FrnsScience/fingerprintguide.pdf*

Forensic Science: Let the Evidence Reveal the Truth
Crime scene evidence and investigation.
http://library.thinkquest.org/04oct/00206/index1.htm

Under the Microscope: Forensics
Facts, games, and video about forensic science.
http://investigation.discovery.com/investigation/forensics/forensics.html

So You Want To Be a Forensic Scientist?
Information about careers in forensic science.
www.aafs.org/choosing-career

▾ INDEX

▾ INDEX

MT. LEBANON PUBLIC LIBRARY